MILLENNIAL INVASION

Discovering Yourself
Through Network Marketing

Jasmine Branford

Millennial Invasion: Discovering Yourself Through Network Marketing

Published by:
10-10-10 Publishing
455 Apple Creek Boulevard
Suite 200
Markham, Ontario
L3R 9X7

Table of Contents

I dedicate this book to you. The millennial who is
feeling stuck on being open to new ideas,
and who wants a laid-out plan to success and is ready
to use network marketing to get uncomfortable
and discover the C.E.O. they've been ready to meet.

Acknowledgments

For years, I never thought that I would become an author, because I hated writing. So, God, I would like to first thank you for showing me my true worth, and for keeping the promises that you've always had for me. Lord, I pray that you continue to live through me, and take me to higher levels as I follow the steps of your son, Jesus Christ.

To my mother, **Debra Seymore,** thank you for all that you do. Your prayers are working. Thank you for being that God-fearing woman that I need in my life. Your love and encouragement are what I needed, every single day, to write the next chapter. The strength that you display on an everyday basis is the reason why I can't give up on my dreams. I am ENOUGH, and it's because you've made me feel nothing less. Thank you for simply being you, my Queen. I love you so much, Mommy; you are truly my best friend.

To my father, **Anthony Branford**, I am so blessed to have you as one of my biggest supporters. Right or wrong, you have always made me feel like I was a winner. Thank you for being the man in my life, to show me how to be loved. Thank you for the push, and for making sure I kept going, writing my book. Without you, Dad, I wouldn't be the woman I am today. Every sacrifice you have made, understand that it will all be worth it. I've got you forever; I love you.

To my one and only sister, **Jenai Branford**, you are my why: why I go hard every single day, and why I challenge myself to be a better version of myself every single day. I know you're watching me, and I pray that God shows you that the Branford sisters will be unstoppable together. I am your keeper, and I will ALWAYS be here for you. I wouldn't dare quit on you, which is why I kept writing. Thank you for being the most caring sister any woman could ask for.

To my brother, **Anthony Branford** (my twin), I adore your competitive spirit. You push me to keep aiming higher, because you're right on my tail. We are 8 years apart, yet you seem to have all of my 25 years of experience. You are so intelligent, and your grind is unstoppable. I AM a proud big sister. Together, we will break our generational curse. Stay focused and true to yourself, because this world is full of distractions. I love you so much; keep grinding.

Thank you, **baby Joshua** and **Toya**! It has only been a year since you made your arrival, and I feel like it's time to go harder. I get to be a better big sister this go around, and I am so blessed for another chance. Your sister is now an author, and it's only the beginning. I love you with all of my heart.

To my family, I want to thank you all for playing a major role in my life: Rosetta Seymore (RIP), Mary Ann Thomas, Camile Thomas, Vaniecia Reaves, David Reaves, Geraldine Eason, Tammy Styles, Shantell Styles, Issetta Johnson, Shanika Hill, Reginald Hill, Iris Fead, Wendell Fead, Juanita Howard, Phillip Seymore, Tommy Howard, Jamelle Howard, Lynette Butts, Quiana Butts, Clyde Butts, Audrey Butts, John Butts, Charles Butts, Francine Butts, Shantae Butts, Tiwan Butts, Quanisha Butts, Marquis Butts, Sherell Butts, Jiyah Butts, Angel Butts, Skylar Butts, Samuel & Denoris King, Tia King-Thomas, Tremia King-Johnson, Samantha King, Tremaine King, Alicia Hester, Roger Hester Jr., Lashanecia Hester, Dorothy Seymore-McRae, Clive Christie Dorreon, Christie Lawrence & Michelle Seymore, Lawrence Seymore, Valeria Seymore, Oliver Seymore, Laurence Seymore, Lamar Seymore, Antonio Young, Michael Cockroft, Barbara Ann King, Clifford Simpson, Demareya Milner, Antonisha Cannon, Clikyerria Simpson.

A big, special thank you to my family in the network marketing industry. As a whole, we are so strong! Without you guys, I wouldn't have had the success that I have today. I am ADDICTED to personal growth, and with these 4years of experience, I am proud to have met every single one of you. With your words of encouragement and support as I transformed into a better woman, I thank God for you all!—David Manning, Shawn Manning, William Thurston (BT Architect), Sunday Chandler, Tajuana and Tony Huston, Nyasha Bangaroo, Jamaal Welch, Thomas (Trey) Harris, Nyzeer Herman, Victor Walker, Kaluah Floyd, David Tinoco (Team Jesus, all day, everyday), Lorna and Briana Harrington, Jackie and Jahla Pippins, JC Oliver, Nichelle Barnes, Heather Williams, Kimberly Jones (Auntie Kim), Kisha King, Treva White, Melissa McNatt, Brittany Turner, Shan Mapp, Loitha Jones, Sunny Ashby, Kim Perkins, Walter Hale, Osbourne and Olayinka (Inky) Lockhart, Dr. Bill and Gayle Thurston, Dardie and Laura Hammie, Maurica Smith, David Guilty, Tiara Mateen, M. Elaine Adkins, Oralee Smith, Renee Young, Sharon D. Anthony, Kevin and Tammy Clayton, Antonio Starr, Erika O'Hara, Andrea Crawford, Ivy Cheatham Baker, Sonic Jones, Kenneth Saunders, Victoria Jackson, Patricia Chandler Williams, Kimberly Johnson, Gary Bonds, Dr. Anissa Jones, Emma Almaraz-Foster, April Brown, Tamera Beasly, Tenaya Maxwell, Brian Nelson, Sean Goldie Bills, Marie Richards, Keasha Johnson, Tasha Fritz Williams, Sherita Daniels (Vacation Rhee Rhee), Justin Thomas, Robin Botts, Shon Glover, Senitra Pritchett, Mary Clemente*, Marlessia Fontaine-Yancey, Bianca Modo Isom, Dionne Anderson, Jarmal Stevens, Andwel Bryant, Leisa Harris, Sabanna Babtiste, JoVaun Gash, Michelle Talmadge, Karen Gresham, Marissa Nelson, Laquinsia Allen, Adrienne Gibbs, Joy Noel Vaughn, Lisa K. George, Trevzie J. Strickland, Christal Clifton, Denise Robinson, Ruth Washington, Sherrie Massie, Marice Smith, Veronica Petty, Timmesha Rogers, Melanie Mitchell, Diane Johnson Freeman, Chris Hunter, Audrey Scott, Michelle Elledge, Michelle Townsend, Claudette Williams, Wendell Campbell, Michelle Adams, India Hughes, Bernice Ryles, Dionne Harris, Peter and Karen Hirsh, Julanda and Timothy George, Kai Solomon, Bridgett Weatherly, Karimah Stewart, Jamial Mumford, Kemp Satchell, Ginger Johnson, Patrice Williams, DL Wallace, Sabrina C. Leon-Cummings, Tajuana Foy Johnson, Athon Clemons, Johnathan Greene, Spencer Iverson, Hollie

Gilmore, Collis Howe, Veronica S. Brown, Donnel Foster Jr.*, Cliffton O'Neal, Tiara Diggs*,Tiffany Bethel, Shaquille Thomas*, Percy Thompson, Nicole Harry, Quincy Walker, Nicole Holder, Natasha Smith, Veda Alexander, Leonard Mailey, Andrea Harris, Tanisha Pope Walker, Michelle Elledge, Oumaima Enk*, Caleb Chandler, Porscha Winley, Yolanda E. Cotton, Tanisha Brown, Mikael and Miranda Masters Van Gogh (Danish power couple) Hardy Robinson, Robyn Sullivan, Lolita Thomas, Melissa Grant, Senetria Pritchett, Jesse Murrah, Deletha Louise Adams, Shawn Johnson, Toiya Arrington, Douglas D. Hampton, Erica Paige, Andre Stewart, Lori Speers, Loe Barber, Adrienne Gibbs, Tanya Greene-Newman, Erin Birch, Daniel R. Watts, Shantrill Sullivan, Sabrina C. Leon-Cummings, Lynett Simmons, Dinah Wyatt, Danielle Vanzandt, and Melissa Mahlum-Geris. I know I'm missing more names, but I thank you all from the bottom of my heart.

Dance Community: You are the balance that I needed in order to still feel alive. Dancing has always been a breath of fresh air, but I'm blessed to have met these few individuals that have motivated me throughout the years: Terronce TJ Estell, Tracsa T.W. Manson, Stacy Brundage, Rodney Doc Ellis, Lanae TJ Thomas, Ser C Andrew Cameron, Judy Sunshine Martin, Adrienne Scott, H. Demetrius Jones, Drewy Alexander, Tony Hearn, Michael A. Fields, Scherlyne Roy, Marty Brogdon, Rhonda Lynn, Kirkpatrick Mitchell, Al Johnson, Donald Cunegin, Maurice Franklin, the entire One Step Above and Soul2Sole organization.

Jerome "Jay" Danzie, thank you for being the first person to see an author in me. When you told me to write a book, I remember looking at you as though you had lost your mind. I went on and on, explaining how I am not a writer, and how I'm not writing any book. Well, friend, here we are, and I am so blessed to have you in my corner. Your support has helped me take another step toward being a better version of me.

To my friends and spiritual influencers, thank you for encouraging me, believing in me, and making me feel enough!—Pastor Jermaine and Nicole Johnson, Miracle Johnson, Christina King Rogers, Lea Bernard, Richard Wilson, Kimya Motley, Yavonee Jones, YaYa Conner, Zuleakha Edwards-Broady, Keischa Bradley, Andrea Beavers, Tierra Major, Shauna Lucas, Antranique Usher, Jeremiah Davidson, Richard Ragland (RIP), Shatika Ricketts, and Katina Johnson. And to the best accountability partners, thank you so much! You all have been so motivating; thank you for your support. Friends like you are hard to come by, and the push was definitely needed—Rebecca Norgaisse, Michael Nickerson, and Denard Curry.

About the Author

Jasmine Branford was born and raised in Miami, Florida, but is currently living in Conyers, Georgia. Being the oldest of four siblings, she's always trying to find new ways to lead by example. After graduating high school, Jasmine attended Georgia State Perimeter College to further her education as a computer science engineer. She was drained from coding and, right before graduating, she knew that this was a career that she was no longer interested in. The funny thing is, Jasmine didn't choose network marketing—it chose her.

With a lack of experience in the beginning, she felt her soul light up from helping others succeed in an industry with plenty of personal development, and that was her new addiction. She's a world traveler, so at any given moment, she can be in a city near you.

The author is available for delivering keynote presentations to appropriate audiences. For rates and availability, please contact Jasmine directly, at info@jasminebranford.com.

To order more books, please visit Amazon.com.

Also, if you have been inspired by *Millennial Invasion*, the best thing you could ever do is pass this along to someone else who's in need of assistance on this journey of success. Be the example of what a leader looks like; together, we can make a difference.

Foreword

I initially met Jasmine Branford when she volunteered to be one of the first people at a *Get Motivated* event, which aimed to help entrepreneurs grow. An eager learner, Jasmine not only chose to take notes, but she kept her engagement and energy levels blazing high as speaker after speaker stepped on stage. As one of the speakers, I noticed Jasmine was among the first to run up to me because she wanted to take her business to the next level. The next level was branding, and that's the topic I had to speak about that day. It's funny because, at the time, she didn't even know how just her contagious presence and high energy levels said a lot about her brand!

When she told me how passionate she was about connecting with younger individuals and helping them to discover themselves through passion and purpose, I immediately knew *Millennial Invasion* is what you, as a young adult, needs to find the missing piece to your success.

It's not every day you see someone so young and determined to live a life that she and every dream-maker deserves through network marketing. I am incredibly impressed with the hard work Jasmine poured into millennial invasion, and all because she wanted to be first! The first to get uncomfortable and chase her dreams, the first to inspire others in her family, and the first to dedicate herself to breaking her family's generational curse.

I've been in the publishing industry for a long time now, and I was very open to Jasmine's idea to develop a book for millennials.

After finishing this book cover to cover in one go, I can definitively say one thing: it is a must-read! Jasmine is all about action. So not only will you read the book, but you will also be able to write down the biggest takeaways that you can apply to your daily life. Not only will you see the simplicity of how network marketing can change your life, but you will also realize the importance of personal development, and understand that this knowledge will take you to a door of no return.

So get ready to clear your mind and get rid of all the old thoughts that were holding you back. I highly recommend Jasmine and *Millennial Invasion.*

Raymond Aaron
New York Times Bestselling Author

Chapter 1

Be First!

"Victorious warriors win first and then go to war, while defeated warriors go to war first and then seek to win."
– Sun Tzu

Live Life in Ownership

Congratulations on being you!

You are a millennial, and you know that your self-worth is outstanding. You are brave, you are bold, and you are coming on strong to other generations. Trust me; it is just the beginning of a life that would be unforgettable. Remember, a few years ago, you used to dream hard. You used to have the wildest imagination.

Like your friends, you honestly believed that after you graduated, everything would come together—like the pieces of a puzzle all falling into place. But now that you are a millennial, ready to live your best days, can you say that your dream has stayed the same? Has life turned out to be the way you thought it would? The good news is that you are young. Do you know what that means? You still have time to get it right! If life hasn't fallen into place like you thought, don't take it as the end of everything. Let me tell you that it is just the beginning.

My question for you is: How soon will you be ready to take full control of your life? The question is simple. I am pretty sure, at this moment, the answer that popped into your head is: NOW. You say you want to take full control of your life right now, but the real question isn't when—it is **how.** So, how are you going to do it?

Being first is the key! You have to be first in all the right ways. Be first in making the decision that is clear and unambiguous. Be first to decide that going back is not an option.

At the age of 21, I had to wake up and see that I never had full control of my life. Ever since I was a newborn, I always had someone telling me what to do. Remember when you first started preschool, or when you began grade school? Do you remember standing in long lines back when you were in high school? If you think about it for a while, you will realize that you have always had someone telling you to do things in your life. People would tell you when you could use the bathroom, when you could have lunch, and of course, when you needed to get your work done. You might have those flashbacks of saying, *"Man, I can't wait to become an adult!"* You said that because you, as a child, thought that you would get to have a say when you grew up. Has that happened to you, though?

If you haven't noticed, as an adult, the cycle of being told what to do has not changed much. In the corporate world—or should I say a regular 9 to 5 job—your life is still dictated by when you can use the bathroom, when you can have a lunch break, and when you can go home. And don't forget that on top of all that, you are expected to be productive on someone else's time! Most of us don't have anything that we can call our own—not even our time.

Can you see how, from the moment you were born, you were already being taught about how society expects you to live as an adult? I will start out by telling you that just because you are a millennial, it doesn't mean that the clock is not ticking for you. Your time is limited, so don't waste a minute living someone else's life. I'm going to ask you simply: Is this really the life for you? Again, can you really say that you have full control of your life? If the answer is yes, then this may not be the book for you. If your answer is no, then you have picked the right guide. You know that you want to learn to live the life you want, with no one else exercising control over you. Keep reading—here, you will find the initial roadmap designed for your freedom.

Invest in You!

As a millennial, I still have those wild imaginations about my future. And so do you. Even though it's all nice and good to dream, the person who starts with only the thought of being wealthy won't go very far. You must have a great ambition to achieve great things. To take full control of your life, you have to be ambitious enough to take action. By taking action, I simply mean investing in yourself.

The practical step is to take the little income that you have now and invest it. Instead of spending your hard-earned money on careless things such as shoes, clothes, jewelry, movies, and video games, why not take those same earnings and learn how to flip one dollar into ten dollars? Let's get one thing straight. The materialistic things that you buy on the weekends are really just to impress the people around you—they have nothing to do with you becoming who you want to be. Spending money on careless items would only create a small leak, which would eventually sink the great ship that your life can become. You're just investing in the sea of sameness. As you buy those things, you become like everyone else. And that will get you absolutely nowhere! You must learn to simply invest your energy into something that is going to contribute to your own growth.

The general idea of investing is to get a high return on income. This is where I will ask you to diverge from the norm: You must start with the investor—that is, yourself. When you invest in yourself, you learn new skills. You discover your talents, the ones that were already stored inside of you from the beginning. Once you have polished your abilities, it will be time for you to serve others and live a life of freedom.

It is no one else's responsibility but your own, to discover your purpose in life and your true happiness. Situations in life will start to align for you from your Provider. This will be one of your greatest returns. You want your mindset to be already aligned with your future of success, because the journey won't be easy. At the same time, though, you can't exclude yourself from the race. So, as a millennial, you owe it to yourself to first understand self-love and self-worth. Do this at the start of your journey of investing in life-changing experiences.

Be first to not only save your money but to invest your money. I like to personally think that my work is not just some boring job. My job is actually being a temporary lender who is helping me invest in my freedom. So when I step foot through the doors of my workplace, I put on my best attitude. And so should you, because you won't be here for long. The next time you clock in, begin to use your job materials to enhance yourself and exercise your talents in that atmosphere. At this very moment, you are living in one of the greatest times that you could be living in.

Like I said earlier, you are bold, you are brave, and your attitude sends a message to other generations. The attitude of millennials is one of courageousness and the willingness to reach their goals! This is the reason that many millionaires are created from the group of millennials, on a monthly basis. My question for you is: Why would you count yourself out? You are just as qualified to join that group of the smart and the successful.

You are qualified to invest in yourself. You are also just as qualified to start taking full control of your life today. You just have to make a decision and then take action. You have to be the first to invest in *you*. Take a moment to visit the bonus section, at MInvasion.com, to see other millennials stepping into the season of boldness. You will find that you are not alone in this teeming-with-potential period of your life that is happening.

Who's in Your Circle?

There is a point in life when you truly start to feel that instant change in your surroundings. The same group of friends that you were very close with in high school may not be those same friends that carry on to your next destination in life. Some people will add to your life, and multiply things in your life; but then there are those that will divide and subtract things from your life. Does your circle of friends speed you up in life? If not, then you've got a problem.

Your friends must be a group of people that inspire you to dream big, aim high, and most importantly, encourage you to not give up. The fact still remains that it doesn't matter how smart you are, how talented you are, or even where you come from. It's just about your work ethics and the army that stands with you to make your vision come true. With time, your real success will show you who your friends are—you can do this just by examining the people that you gave most of your time to.

I remember my graduation night; my best friends and I all crowded around each other, ready to take pictures, wearing our black and red gowns. We tossed our caps in the air to capture the perfect image of closing a chapter of our lives and opening a new one. We were all jumping and screaming, looking forward to starting our new journey as we celebrated the entire night with family and classmates. Surprisingly, we had all attended different schools. It was the first fall break when I started to notice new attitudes, new behaviors, and unrecognizable topics in our conversations. In the beginning, I couldn't understand how five-plus years of friendships could easily fall apart, or how ten-plus years of friendships could effortlessly begin to fade. It amuses me to this day because I remember how large my circle used to be. Now, my circle is just a line segment of two of my closest peers, who I started with from the beginning.

I remember back when I thought it was my friends who were changing, when honestly, it was me all along. I was growing into a new person. I tried to backtrack and fix things because I wasn't a fan of drama, but my Provider had already decided to teach me the hard way. It led me to the door of no return. As life continued, I started to discover more of my wants and desires. The more I started to focus on the goal, the more I felt myself being pulled to a newer circle.

You want to be the millennial who is different from the public that hasn't yet discovered their worth. So, it's important that you choose your associations based on your destiny. Never keep the company of anyone that doesn't improve you or contribute to making you better. The older you get in years, the more you begin to see the straight path of where you want to go in life. If you are going to hunt elephants, don't get off the trail for a silly rabbit, and if you are going to fly with eagles, don't descend for a moment to spread your wings and fly with the pigeons. Your friends must reach your level or higher.

Right now, you may not understand it, but as you step into the process, it will hurt a little bit. Earlier, you didn't realize that the majority of your circle was not really getting you anywhere; these were the people who always wanted you to go with them quickly. Keep a little distance from those "what are you doing," or "WYD," friends. Once your time becomes limited for your acquaintances, the shift will begin. But believe me when I say that this adjustment won't be bad at all. It is simple if you want to be the first in your circle to have full control of your life. Start hanging around individuals who already have that full control as a millennial.

Breaking the Curse from Wages to Wealth

The world is changing rapidly. Even though time has its own pace, I would say that the millennials have their own! Millennials are moving so fast that they are destined to break the curse of living from paycheck to paycheck. Do you know what it means to live from one month's paycheck to the next? It means that you are managing money by living on only one source of income. You are creative in so many ways, so why do you want to waste your creativity sitting behind a desk, helping another man's dream come to life?

You, like the majority of the population, were told to live a normal life. After school, you were told to go to college, get a degree, and of course, find yourself a J. O. B. In this day and age, unfortunately, life is no longer that easy. The old tried-and-tested path will only give you a lifestyle of being just over broke. Take a look back at your family's history, and ask yourself if you see a pattern of wealth. Do you really think that the key to success and having full control of your life is learning while leaning on only one job? If your grandparents are still working, then what time do you think you will have to live the best days of your life? If your parents are still working, do you actually believe that you will retire before 30? It's possible for you to make a lot of income, but in this book, I need you to comprehend how to make residual income. Residual income is getting paid repeatedly after the work is done. Think of it as royalty checks. Can you imagine going to your job only one time, and your boss pays you over and over after completing that one task? It sounds impossible, but it's definitely accomplishable. It will happen to you when you make the decision to become your own boss and create your own rules.

From the time I graduated, I have always had a passion for math. So, I invested in a career that I hoped would put me above the poverty line. I studied computer science, expecting to make $83,000 a year. At 21 years old, that was an excellent salary for me. However, later on that year, I met a gentleman in the network marketing industry, who

7

was earning an income of $83,000 a month. Get this: He made more in a month than I did in the entire year! I got the shock of my life. I started to see that there were alternate ways of getting where I wanted to be in life.

During this period, my mind changed radically. Watching the successful people around me, I decided that I was not going to count myself out. I wanted to be as successful as I could be too. My grandmother introduced me to the network marketing industry. This was the time when I started to experience entrepreneurship at a faster level. It was my first in corporate America. Pretty soon, I realized that bonuses and raises were the hardest rewards to come by. It was when I had my first experience in network marketing that I got to know what it felt like to give myself an $8,200 bonus.

I am not going to lie; it most definitely stroked my ego just a little, because for the first time in my life, I felt like I was on the path to finally breaking the family curse of living from check to check. After examining your family's history, are you bold enough to step up and break your family's curse? Even if you come from a background of living above the poverty line, you are not financially free until your family has full control of all their income. It is entirely possible to have six figures this year, and have four figures the following year. As long as another man is controlling the income that flows into your household, you, my friend, have yet to experience true financial freedom. Be the first in your circle to tap into the wealth system. Be the first to unlock the doors of earning from a minimum of 7 different streams of income.

F.E.A.R.

As you continue to progress on this road, be aware of your thoughts. Your brain is a muscle that can play multiple roles. One role that your brain is strictly designed to perform is to protect you. So, when you try to step out of your comfort zone to improve your future, it's easy for your mind to talk you out of a lot of things. In today's world, the majority will call it *fear*.

F. E. A. R. is merely *False Evidence Appearing Real.*

Just like any other muscle in your body, you have to train your brain to create new thoughts and accept new challenges. The good thing is that fear is actually a great thing. I say that because where there is fear, there is courage as well. The next time you start to have new ideas, it should scare you just a little bit. Take it as a litmus test—it will help you know that your faith is being challenged. With courage, you will simply be inspired to move. So you move at an uncomfortable pace when fear is becoming existent in your life—and again, that is a great thing!

Let me just say that you are designed to be successful in life. Think of your life as a seed that was planted the moment that you were born; know that you were specifically planted to blossom into a tree. Every tree and living thing has a purpose. To fulfill that purpose, they have to go through a process. So do you. When it comes to business, I would be lying if I said that the process will be easy. It will be simple, but it won't be the easiest route you take in life.

In life, you have to be willing to accept new challenges. It is a necessary step to take if you want to change your circumstances. You are a millennial who wants more; you are a millennial who wants to set an example; you are a millennial who wants to be the first to break that family curse! You are taking on a big challenge. And as I find you here, seeking more knowledge from this book, I already know that you will succeed. So, as a brand-new investor that wants to take full control of their life, understand that there will be a few bumps in the road. There are going to be times when procrastination will win the fight. However, know that your original plan that day was going to get you ahead. When you hold a vision so strong to take on a big task, you should not let the distractions slow you down. Keep up your momentum while your energy is still positive and high, because the reward will be so sweet at the end! You deserve to know the taste of it.

Don't let fear slow you down on what you have been called to do. Don't let fear stop you from living your life to the best of your ability. Don't let fear control your dreams. F. E. A. R., in the words of Tony Robbins, and my clean version is *Forget Everything and Run*. So, put on your track shoes now, because your future is waiting for you!

You must learn to live with, as well as benefit from, fear. Remember, you are the creator, and the creator has just as much courage as a lion! If you let fear step in your way, the most significant pain that you will ever feel is the pain of regret. So learn the self-discipline that you need when it comes to your success. Know that you, too, can be the voice for other millennials who also want to succeed, just like you.

Every Step Counts! M.A.D. Millennial

Understand that you are not just here to gain knowledge but to apply it. Let this book guide you to fully become the successful millennial that you already are. My job is to help you, because I want you to win. Get mad, and know that your season is coming; because now, you are the investor who is sowing seeds in your future.

Now that you have completed Chapter one, what are some takeaways that you got from this chapter? Remember, for you to really succeed in life, you must first take action! My advice to you is to simply get mad! M.A.D. means *make a decision*. You are now qualified to be a M.A.D. millennial. Take a few moments to write down some takeaways as you progress to the next chapter. Don't wait too long, because Chapter 2 is going to be another step to get you closer to your freedom.

Chapter 2

You Must Retire Young!

"If you start working in your twenties and retire at age sixty, you may spend as many years in retirement as you did working."
– Michael Bivona

New Journey to Independence

Being successful means aiming high and working hard to live a life that has always been a dream. Going to college allows you to start on that dream independently, and that's a big stepping stone for most. The longevity of your success during these years will be the most challenging task of all.

It's a fact that the person you were, when you first stepped foot on your college campus for the first time, won't be the same individual graduating down the line. As you begin a new chapter, you might get a bit nervous. However, you knew it was time for a change, so you exited that stage. During the four years, it was time for you to truly identify yourself. The power of it all was networking with each other to see what sparked your interest. You were exposed to new information and philosophies from your peers. In doing so, you found out the things that could make *you* a better you. There were countless days and nights when you experienced the rush of hanging out with your friends, partying in the frat house until the sun came up. You also learned what your first hangover in class felt like, from the unforgettable memories from homecoming. All of these experiences were thrilling, but keep in mind that for any college student, there are days where they come up short to buy the book they need for class, or for the better food they want to eat because they finally experienced "Freshman 15." Many times, it must have happened that you couldn't financially afford to do those things.

What if there was a way to make passive income while attending school? All that time that you had to party and go out, wouldn't it be worthwhile if you used a bit of that time to invest in a business that allowed you to make extra income, without having to always work physically? These sources of income are online and will give you a chance to work remotely. Studying and getting a clear focus on where you want to be in your future can already seem like a full load. However, earning residual income, at the same time, not only raises your belief but gives you options. And everyone loves to have more than one opportunity at their disposal.

When I was in college, I was very tight with my money, and I never dared to ask my parents for cash. It was one rainy afternoon when I was stressed out from calculus class that I got a call from my grandmother. She repeatedly said to me, *"You need to get yourself business, and you need to bring in some extra money now!"* I must say that she called on a good day, because that was the day when my college life was more stressful than exciting.

Although I had a plan to become successful after graduating, at that very moment, I needed money. It was hard to focus when college dues and domestic bills were the only things on my mind. As my grandmother rambled on, with her mentor on the line, I heard her say one thing: *"Get paid to travel."* When your mindset gets into entrepreneur mode, your creativity starts to spark as quickly as possible. The same happened to me. As I talked to my grandmother, my mind was telling me to launch spring break for my classmates. I wasn't as social as I should have been, so I printed off these colorful, bright flyers to promote a spring break cruise. That's where I started. That's the point where my clientele started growing.

Can you see your college years getting slightly more relaxing as you find a way to earn income? How are you utilizing your current social circle? Is it helping you improve your current circumstances? Sharing your website with different clubs, organizations, and social groups will be one of the most effective ways of making some money in your sleep.

Was College Your Only Option?

By the time we graduate from high school, the school system has already prepped us from the beginning to take tests and prepare ourselves to go to college. You have been continuously taking exams every week since grade 1, to see if you were even qualified to attend a university. But let me ask you this: Did these tests really dictate your future? What we don't know is that there's more to life than a piece of paper and trying to determine where we should be. The school system doesn't know what you dream about at night. When you close your eyes, what do you think about over and over again? Can you really read about it? Is it already in a textbook? And can a test really determine what your future should look like? Growing up the way I did, I thought the traditional route was the only way to take if I wanted to have a secure life.

For instance, my parents always told me to do better than them. Doing better, from that perspective, meant me going to school, making good grades, getting that diploma, going off to college for free, and securing a job that paid me well for as long as I worked at it. That was the only path that I knew would take me to success. It was my capital "A" plan, and my lowercase "a" plan as well.

No one told me that there was another way for me to live a successful life, and I thought that college was the only way to succeed.

As a M.A.D. millennial, do you realize how many millionaires are coming into existence on a daily basis, with only a high school education? Better yet, do you know that there are plenty of millionaires today who never even finished high school? Think long and hard of the odds of people actually graduating college just for them to be working at their careers today. The odds are very, very slim. Think about it now: What was your path? I remember when I first got introduced to the network marketing industry; I met a lot of young millennials who were very successful. Would you believe that many of them barely graduated from high school, and very few of them had even graduated from college? I, on the other hand, had attended and graduated from college.

While getting my college degree was one of my greatest accomplishments, I had already made the decision that my field was just not for me. Not everyone wants to be a statistic and stick to the book. There are people like myself—the ones that are not afraid to take an alternate route. I discovered that my peace of mind was more important to me. And I understood that peace wouldn't come till I was living my true purpose.

Here's Your Student Loan

When I first got started in my network marketing company, I saw a lot of millennials becoming successful in this so-called "pyramid." Well, it wasn't until I essentially discovered what a true pyramid was that I understood what it was all about. I found out that these individuals had decided to take a risk. I finally discovered their story of ultimate success. These were people who were, in many ways, just like me, yet they had these incredible success stories. Some of these individuals, as I said, were not even college graduates.

Keep in mind that I am not encouraging you to be a high school dropout; nor do I intend to stop you from attending college to get more knowledge. I'm just simply telling you that you have the same possibilities of success as those other people. In fact, you have those opportunities at this very moment, and you should be excited! The ones that I have seen, at the top of my industry, all had a low education level. It was titled "low" because of what society had decided to title them as. However, did their education really mean so little, compared to the success that they had over the years?

In continuation, I learned over the years that it is not about the education that you find in the books. Self-education can be the most powerful tool that you can have.

Success Story #1

One of my closest business partners decided that she was going to college, and she was going to study to get a degree in the line that she had already been involved in from the age of 16 years old. In time, however, she realized that after attending school, it didn't make sense to keep pushing for a mere piece of paper to define her success. The income she made today would grow expeditiously without a college degree, and she discovered that early.

So, here's what she did: She gave her mom an ultimatum. I am sure this ultimatum had to be made because her mom thought that going to college and having a degree would make a big difference in her life. Like other people from the older generation, her mom thought that a college degree would define her daughter's success. So this young lady decided to challenge the old ideas that her mother still clung to.

She said to her mom, *"I promise I can make more income if I work my current job than I would if I finished college earning my degree."* She told her mom that if she was able to achieve this goal within a year, she would have to accept that her daughter no longer had to attend college.

How many individuals, under the age of 21, can say that they are making over $75,000 to $90,000 a year? Well, this is what this young lady was able to do within a year and so on. She showed that she could make way more income than she would make if she finished those four years of college. She demonstrated that it was not only about what you know; it's all about your work ethic and who you know.

My Student Loan to You

Here's my student loan to you: Understand your self-worth, and decide to give yourself the right education. Understand that you are just as valuable when you put your hard work into any project. If you want to be a successful millennial, my student loan to you is to go out and get your hands dirty. Go out and actually get involved in your career. Go out and learn how to network, and also learn the crucial skill of accepting the word, *no*.

Once you get through that phase, you will get to the place where you can produce income based on your efforts—not based on what a piece of paper and what another human being tells you to do. So, do you really want to have a relationship with Sallie Mae, or do you really want to build that relationship with yourself, so that you, too, can produce an income that a lot of your peers didn't know was possible? You have the option of understanding the value of self-worth and hard work, versus having to continuously stress yourself about completing an essay, graded to show you your worth on the scale A–F. The decision is yours to make.

Stop Hallucinating!

"A wise mentor once told me that a dream
without a plan is just a hallucination."
– W. Thurston

A lot of millennials finish high school, thinking that they will go to college to pursue a dream. The reason that most never graduated with a degree that they intended to get was that they were hallucinating the entire time. You may be one of those people. Can you admit that the reason was that you never did what was required? You maybe didn't even know what was required. What you really needed to do was to actually map out your future, and make it as detailed as you would for a business plan. You thought you had it all figured out, until you realized how tough it was going to be.

So, did you prep yourself to understand what the process would be like? Indeed, we never know what the process is going to be before we start. In our heads, we think that it is going to be a nice, simple, and smooth ride. But in reality, we go through the ups and downs, and we go through the trials. It is because the person you want to meet, out of this whole season, is not going to be the same person that you knew before you decided to take this step forward.

What we normally do is that we get a little scared. We get a little shaken up because it's different, and nobody has truly molded us and prepped us for what is about to take place before we can get the success that we want to receive. My advice to you is to stop hallucinating. Stop waking up every day with wishful thinking, hoping that your success is just going to fall into your lap. Success doesn't come that quickly or easily. In reality, you are supposed to meditate about it and work for your success daily. You are supposed to map your entire success plan out! If you come home with a new idea or a better path of success, or if you came back home feeling fresh and renewed, then congratulations! You are now watering the seed that you planted, maybe days ago, weeks ago, months ago, or even years ago.

Try to examine your success as a tree. It sounds silly, but understand that roots have to first stretch deep down into the dark rich soil for the tree to grow. It started with the seed, but with the right daily treatment to make it grow, that seed will become unrecognizable. That's how you have to look at your success. What this means is, did you fall down a few times to get back up? Have you experienced the humiliation and the pain that made you want to quit, but you didn't? You think you're going hard now, but when was the last time you pushed yourself until your actions became unrecognizable? You have what it takes, and you owe it to yourself to find new versions of yourself by simply doing what's required every day.

It's easy for us to say things. But if you haven't mapped it out on paper, where do you think your success path is going to take you? Are you serious about your future, or are you hallucinating? What do you really see when you close your eyes? Have you arrived at your destination when you close your eyes, or are you still trying to get yourself out of the fog? Don't be the millennial that tells false dreams to themselves, only because you are unclear about the outcome.

Your Future Depends on You

Mad millennial, what I really need you to do at this point is to get a better understanding of what you really want to achieve in life. Don't be the person who only knows that one old path that so many people have already walked. For example, it shouldn't really be your goal to aim for a degree for four years, just to achieve an associate's job and to prove to outsiders that you are as qualified as them or just above average.

In reality, most students waste years trying to please everyone else but themselves. That habit initially came from wanting to be accepted by society. But following the herd will not take you closer to achieving your goals. Being extremely ambitious, I personally began to lose myself when I went down the conventional path. I didn't want to seem ungrateful because, at the time, I was taking in all this knowledge without having to take out a student loan. However, I realize that the time cost me way more than the income that it took to take those classes.

You see, your future really depends on you. It is up to you now on how soon you really want to start living out your dreams. It is easy for you to go out and party and be just like those other college students who just want to claim that they're "living their best life." The truth, however, is that they perform these actions to hide the real concern. These millennials are crying out to take a break from growing up. How can I blame them if the majority wasn't prepared to deal with adulthood and its accompanying responsibilities? However, you have the potential to change the general perception. You can be a leader who is living proof to their peers—proof of all that is possible to achieve for this generation. So, what do you want? Do you want to put in the hard work right now so that you can live life to its fullest, or do you just want to invest in the life of being average? Though it appears otherwise, the normal life that you think is safe, is going to cost you way more. But of course, the decision is up to you.

Again, your future depends on you. This means that your life, your decisions, and your actions are going to make a path of what your future is going to look like for you. The activities of your friends or your peers, and the habits of your associates, will make no difference, because it's not their life—it's your life! Take a step further to remove yourself out of the picture.

Understand that others depend on you to break the cycle for freedom. Would you at least do it for your bloodline, or for the person who looks up to and admires you because, in their eyes, you are their hero? Don't let people down, who carry hope and faith with them every day, waiting to witness another way to early retirement.

Now, my question to you is, what are you going to do about it?

Some of you have already realized that you didn't have it all figured out, and it's back to the drawing board. If you have already been measuring your successes, and are very clear on what your future looks like, then congratulations! Start challenging yourself. Make it a point to never become too comfortable with your success, because there is always more for you to achieve. Every day when you walk out of your house, you should come home richer than you were before. It does not have to be financially richer; it can be as simple as learning a new thing—because the more you learn, the sooner you will earn.

Ask yourself if you took the time to learn something new today. Did you take the time to apply your knowledge today? Did you take the time to teach back that knowledge today? If you have not tried to do those top three things daily, what are you really living for? What are you actually achieving as you go from day to day? What did you really get done today?

Aim to break the cycle of repeating the day that you have had many times before. How many days are you going to keep repeating day one? How many times are you going to keep repeating, year after year, just to realize that you're stuck? Time is money, and money is time. Increase your worth, and keep pace with time. Remember, the clock keeps ticking.

M.A.D. millennial, you're ready for Chapter 3!

Once again, you are not just here to gain knowledge but to apply it. Take a few moments to write down some takeaways as you progress to the next chapter. Don't wait too long, because Chapter 3 will get you to the next step—one more step closer to your freedom.

Chapter 3

Fast Money, Really?

*"You get quick money, it's beautiful, there's sunshine,
but at the end of the day, you find out it's all a masquerade, baby.
It's not what it seems."*
– Wyclef Jean

There is No Such Thing!

Every day, your life consists of waking up to make a living, and what living can you really bring to existence without money? Growing up, you have created your personal beliefs on what money really is. In my house, money did not grow on trees! Every store visit was a drag as we desperately reached for that sparkling item, with longing.

Sometimes we could afford everything we wanted; at other times, we couldn't even afford the things we needed.

You can change all of that!

Why?

Because you are a millennial.

Now, you may be wondering what exactly that entails. Does that mean that you can have everything you desire for free? Does that mean that money magically appears under your pillow? Or does that *imply* that there are multiple ways open to *you* to make more money in less time?

I would go with the final option!

As a millennial, you have a multitude of opportunities open to you. You can make a huge amount of income in a short space of time, only because you were born in an age where you have been learning since the day you were born.

As millennials, you have more skills than you think!

Let's take a look at some of the skills that you already have up your sleeve.

Millennials Are Fast!

You may have noticed that you tend to pick things up quite quickly. Whether it was learning to operate your first tablet or using your first smart phone, you could do it by the age of 2!

What's the reason behind it?

You're a millennial!

You have been exposed to the digital world since before you were born. That makes things all the more interesting for you. Not only that, you are the problem solvers of this age.

Why not use this untapped potential to grow in life?

Scam Versus Business

The second most important skill that you have is that you can identify a scam versus a business. As a millennial, once again, your exposure comes into play. You have seen so much from such a young age, only because you have access to the internet. You are aware of the global market as well as your local resources.

You can easily determine whether a particular deal that you're trying to finalize is an actual business or a scam. A real business opportunity can help you realize all your dreams. From a second perspective, some people may call the business that you have started, a scam, even when it's not. Beware of such false blemishes on the work that you do.

Because you are a millennial, you have a fresh mindset when it comes to business and investment. Investing in network marketing today allows you to invest low to receive a high return, but do you actually know the difference?

Once you start getting into the flow of things, you're going to realize that the same people you thought were your friends, will soon become haters; because in reality, they would be the last people who would want to join forces with you.

Many people from older generations feel a bit insecure about millennials, only because they can do so much more at such a young age. Such options were unavailable for the older generations when they were young.

The fast pace at which millennials grow can make people envy them.

Heads up!

There's going to be this funny little word that people might use for your business: *scam*. But do you honestly know what a scam refers to in network marketing?

Well, let me help you out. A scam is a business that has absolutely no product. So if you're going to have a referral program, and you're going to recruit someone, what are you actually recruiting for? Is this person just a number, or do they have a role to provide to the public as well? Does the company even provide anything to the public?

You will want to know what kind of profit the company makes, to determine if it's a fair business or a scam. In a scam, businesses don't succeed. They provide a service that doesn't actually end up giving any benefits to the general public.

Your business is not like that! If you have a business that adds value to people and society at large, then you can show people that you have something authentic for them!

Your business must have a cycle of money that keeps on rotating, and every individual member of your business must get enough to meet their needs. If only the upper hierarchy of your business makes money, and the people at lower levels feel like they're not making enough, then your business suffers losses, because then you have a dissatisfied team working with you.

What if your product was travel?

It is the largest industry in the world, which allows you to make income from something that you were going to do anyway. What if your product was something in the weight loss field? What if your product was something that helps you build your mindset as an entrepreneur, empowering you and allowing you to give back to your community?

You can even go for a business that provides multiple streams of service. For instance, if you provide traveling packages that help consumers save, how fun would that be? Every time someone you know saved on a trip, you got paid, and the best part is that you gave away these discounts for free.

The simplicity will attract those with the desire to travel, to your business, and you will also be able to make more profits!

So, when people complain to you that your business is a scam, be sure to educate them and give them an idea about what a scam is, and how your business is giving valuable services and products to people.

So, what type of business do you know that you can actually do? If you get stuck about making the right choice, visit MInvasion.com today, to get different ideas about your prospective business, and how they will benefit you.

You will be able to see that such businesses never get old or outdated. They never run out of style. So when you put yourself in a position to invest, you can be a part of something that gives back to the public, something that the public can feed off of. I want you to understand that you then have a true business, no matter what product or service you're dealing in, because scam opportunities don't contribute to making a difference at all. So, in the words of our millennials today, "Stay woke."

Think of your network marketing franchise as a Walmart store that provides tools, services, and products. When you learn how to leverage people's money, and get them addicted to the services you provide, you officially enter the winning circle. You have a legitimate business—no scams! Besides having the right skills, you also have the capability to gain high returns, from very little investments. Let's see how you can do that.

Low Investment, High Return!

Everyone wants to make more profits by investing in small costs in the world today. That's no secret.

The ideology of the world is shifting toward the idea of profiting without needing to put so many seeds in the ground. Can you imagine just planting one seed, and that one seed sprouting up to where it's always going to produce fruits? As a young millennial, only you can do that.

Do you want to live a rewarding lifestyle? Well, sometimes it doesn't have to take multiple seeds to be able to produce just as many fruits. It just takes that one investment for you to be able to produce those multiple streams that you have already intended to get in your future. You see, the best thing about you being young is that you already understand that the majority of us were not born rich, which is why we can only invest a little amount into our business venture.

Like everyone who wants to be successful, we try to make sure that our investment gives us returns in the millions. There are many millennials in the world who have already achieved this. So can you!

For instance, at the age of 21, as a college student, I only had one source of income. That was when I got introduced to my first network marketing company.

Can you believe that my remuneration at the time was only a hundred and fifty dollars per month? It is nothing compared to the expenses we have to take care of in the world that we live in today—just a pair of shoes can cost us about a hundred and fifty dollars. The same goes for the clothes that we buy, or for the groceries that need to last for a week.

When you earn so little, you keep questioning yourself: How are you adding anything to your household? If you invest the same amount of money in a particular business, you at least have a chance of multiplying it.

Learn how to put your future first. Keep aside the money that you were going to spend on drinks and food with your friends; you can actually use that to make investments that would lead to profits.

Many people open their businesses by borrowing a large sum of money. Opening a business on credit is not something that would benefit you or your business; in fact, it would add to your liabilities.

You are a millennial, and as a result, smart working is what you must do!

So, find yourself a business that's going to be online, because that is where you always are, and you will earn passive income. Can you imagine being that millennial who can go to sleep at night and make an income while they dream in their slumber?

The internet doesn't sleep; it stays up 24 hours a day. Doesn't it make sense to you to invest in something that does not shut down?

You spend the majority of your time, every day, on social media. Why not learn how to make income from a tool that's never going to shut down?

Some of the most prominent billionaires in the world do this every single day. People are making low investments in stocks alone, and making huge returns as a result. They have been living a luxurious life for years.

Why break the cycle? If they're rich and are already using this strategy successfully, we can do it too! Why pick up poor habits when using your money? Instead of just spending, why not take the little that you have, and learn how to use it productively.

That way, you can have that success in the form of riches as well. I need you to think about what a low investment is for you—one that can produce a high return.

I've witnessed it way too many times in my industry. Teens are taking a chance, and investing their last savings into low-income investments. But they can produce twice as much—and thrice as much, and four times as much.

As a coach, I will be able to guide you to make more than the average individual. You'll be ahead of most, because you, my friend, will have a second source of income, and that will lead to more open doors. These doors will be able to generate income to support your entire household, with the residual amount in your pocket!

Take a few moments to write down some takeaways as you progress to the next chapter. Don't wait too long, because Chapter 4 will get you to the next step—one more step closer to your freedom.

Chapter 4

See the World! It's Your Playground

"You are not here merely to make a living. You are here in order to enable the world to live more amply, with greater vision, with a finer spirit of hope and achievement. You are here to enrich the world, and you impoverish yourself if you forget the errand."
– Woodrow Wilson

When was the last time you ever took some time to discover how you manage to work after a break?

The world is a gift that allows you to connect your spirit to what's really in tune with what you really want to pursue. In life, connecting with the spirit is one of the most powerful tools, and unfortunately, the world that we live in today can easily prevent us from exploring ourselves.

Take a good look around you. The world has taught us to make a living for ourselves and our families. We stay busy almost all the time. We barely have any time to look into the mirror and determine what suits our looks the most.

Our work, as well as our families, keeps us busy all the time. As a result, we barely get the time to see what we're doing with ourselves. We never realize how important it is for us to travel around the globe and see the world as it is, so that we can learn from the experiences we go through on those travels.

You may already have a desire to see the world, but you generally ignore it because you are brought up to work more, and to focus on making a living for yourself and your family. As a result, you tend to overlook the fact that you must see the world as it is.

In fact, you spend half your life in conflict because your heart tells you to travel, while your mind asks you to stay put and continue working. So, when do you really have the time just to step away from the world and fully focus on yourself without any distractions?

Traveling can do that for you. It is one of those gateways that are going to allow you to refocus and help you figure out who you are, which is why everyone must travel at least two to three times within a year.

Now, all of you may not have the budget to travel that frequently, but you can utilize several options to satisfy your traveling needs. Join social groups, or plan your traveling trips with your neighbors. With such tricks, you will be able to save a lot of money on your travels.

I have personally traveled a lot in my life, and for quite some time now, I have been traveling at least once a month. My parents gave me the wonderful habit of traveling. They used to take me on family vacations quite often.

I remember, when I was only six or seven years old, I went on a cruise for the first time in my life. Ten years later, I was having the time of my life, taking my first trip overseas to Paris. I had seen the Eiffel Tower up close only then. At 16 years of age, back in 2010, my mom gave me an ultimatum to visit the tower with my classmates, for a period of 10 days.

Because of that ultimatum, I was able to discover so many things about the world. At the time, I was the only one in my neighborhood who had seen the tower, live, in all of its glory. It was such a mind-blowing experience.

After returning from my 10-day trip overseas, I realized that I was always going to connect my soul with the world by simply going back to the Eiffel Tower, or just visiting other places.

That experience helped me come to terms with the fact that I had reached that point in my life where traveling had become compulsory.

Certain moments in your life are simply game changers for you. Such moments are precious. They can be breathtaking and can make you truly appreciate life. They help you to feel grateful for how far you have come in life and how fast you are moving.

Because of these moments, we are able to remember the things that we are grateful for. Generally, we don't stop to appreciate all the good things that happen to us. However, such experiences make us who we are. They give us things that help us to shape our future.

When our spirit fully connects with the world, in our travels, we attain a kind of clarity that helps us in making correct decisions. Travelling doesn't just keep us well-informed about world trends; it also helps in creating unforgettable experiences for us, which gives us personality and character.

As a result, whatever we do becomes magnificent. As millennials, we are fast learners. The things you and I can learn on a week-long trip are some of the most unfathomable things that most people can't even grasp in years.

The power of traveling the world lies in the fact that it helps you attain a state of peace that is quite unachievable otherwise. It is one of the most significant gifts that you can give to yourself.

Once you get used to traveling around a lot, you will be able to do it two to three times a year. Can you imagine the number of possibilities that would become available for you at this pace? Who would you become in that kind of time? Do you have a desire to travel? Do you realize why a lot of us don't even know what path we should take, because we never stood still long enough to focus on ourselves? Take your time, but do take the first step to progress just as well. Hear how travel has helped a college student progress in the world we live in.

Success Story #3

I absolutely love traveling! It is one of the most peaceful and tranquil things one can do. It's great for the soul. To get away and see the world means so much to me. So many people do not realize that there is so much world out there for us all to see. They make excuses and come up with reasons that it's not possible. It's possible if you just put your mind to it. Decide where you want to go, and depending on your funds, when it is feasible. It could be in the next upcoming weeks, months, or years. Just be sure to save up each paycheck, even if it's only a little here and there.

I am a freelance theatre artist, and I have been fortunate to travel to several places across the east coast and out of the country, and to take my work with me. I started taking advantage of traveling in college; it helped me create friendships, network, and generate further opportunities for travel because of the people I was able to meet and/or work with. After college, I continued to travel, and for the most part, I just used to up and go. I would save money and then, in a very short time span, decide to travel to a place. This spontaneity had a big effect on my life. It gave me the ability to just do things and not hesitate, and to ignore the doubts and fears that arose. Seeing the world is important to me because it reminds me that there is so much to see and experience. It also reminds me that we can do whatever we want to do, as long as we put our minds to it! To me, to travel is to live!

– J. Davidson

Take a step forward to leave the comfort of your home. The next time you take a vacation, make sure it's feeding your spirit, and make sure you are reflecting on things that you are grateful for.

Find the True Definition of You

My grandmother introduced me to this idea for the first time in my life. She said that I had to discover the true definition of me.

At the time she had said this to me, I hadn't fully understood what she had been saying. However, after my travels, I got the real gist of her words.

After a while, I understood how exploring the world allows you to explore yourself. Everything that you discover during your travels will eventually become a part of who you are. When I had taken a few trips, I came to the conclusion that what I wanted was to get paid to travel.

I never went back to the Eiffel Tower; not because I didn't want to but because that was something that wouldn't pay me for my travels.

I was ready to start living off my vision, which was to see the world and make money from the experience at the same time. I started my journey from the Bahamas, and finally ended it back in New York and LA. And in between, who can forget the wonderful Punta Cana?

I was able to redefine myself because of my extensive travels around the globe.

During the initial few years of my education, I kept thinking that I was the kind of person who would be comfortable working in a cubicle all my life, since I was a computer science student. However, after my travels, I discovered that I was a social butterfly. I enjoy going out, and greeting and meeting people. I feel fascinated by different cultures and societies.

That's when I made up my mind that sitting at a desk all day long was not something I could do for the rest of my life. I needed a job that allowed me greater interaction with other human beings.

In the nick of time, I understood that I was a much better coach than anything else. Coaching came to me naturally, because I had a treasure trove of experiences to share with my students. I came to terms with the fact that I was a social butterfly. I genuinely felt the need to touch every individual I met during my journey, at a deeper level.

I wanted to seek out and touch everyone's soul.

And how could I do that without adding travel to my lifestyle? What do you want to do? Do you still have dreams? Do you still have desires? Do you still try to take the necessary measures every day to fulfill them? How do you know where your final destination is going to be? Do you even know if there's going to be a final destination in your life? You might just enjoy traveling for the rest of your life.

You may never feel comfortable settling down at a single place in the world.

For instance, when I first traveled to Punta Cana, at the age of 21, I never knew what an all-inclusive trip it would be for me. When I was there, I simply had the time of my life. I woke up every morning expecting just about anything. I could smell the tasty omelet on the stove, and I could anticipate eating anything and everything for lunch for the rest of the day. When I fully realized what kind of freedom this was, it made me feel liberated in a way that I had never felt before.

It was an absolutely blessed period of my life. My only regret was that I didn't have my entire family with me so that we could enjoy everything together. But I knew that I was in the right place at the right time. I knew that the Universe was at my disposal, and if I wanted to keep seeing the world and giving myself a luxury lifestyle, without even having a college degree, I could do it. I knew that the things I truly desired were quite possible to achieve. But getting to this point took long nights. Looking out from my balcony and watching the ocean flowing away endlessly, I realized that I wanted that too. I really wanted to flow away just as seamlessly.

It was as if I had learned a secret to success during my travels. I learned that in order to connect with the world, I had to feel it first. I could do that by listening to the sounds of the ocean from my balcony, or by walking on the beach to feel the thrashing of the waves and the silence of the winds.

You have to listen intently to what the winds have to tell you, and meditate. Meditation helps more than anything. That way, you will be able to feel the energy of the earth around you. While you're at it, you can ask yourself questions, such as what's my purpose, what's my destiny, or even, who am I?

The idea behind your travels must be to keep yourself away from distractions. When you have minimal or no distractions in your life, you will be able to focus more on your goals in life, and as a result, ensure that you succeed at everything you do.

Take this as a challenge, and travel the world as much as you can!

Make Your Savings Your Earnings

For young millennials, savings can be their earnings.

You only have to avoid a few things to make that happen.

Alright, you don't really have a job except for your summer breaks, so you don't earn a lot of money right now. However, your parents give an allowance.

Many people your age tend to spend that allowance on extravagance that doesn't benefit them at all. As a result, they end up spending everything they have, without any idea of how they're going to get it back.

We can indulge all day in the tricky details about how you should spend your money, and it won't be enough. However, I would like to give you a simple tip to save more money and spend less on unnecessary things.

I understand that when you see your friends' Facebook statuses, you feel the need to catch up with the things that they're doing, so that you can continue to be a part of them.

However, senseless spending doesn't have to be a part of what you do every day just so that you can feel accepted by your friends.

Most of the time, you end up spending more than you actually make. You don't do it intentionally, but there are times when you can barely remember that saving is more important than spending money. At other times, you don't have any option but to spend to fulfill your household needs. But even in that case, you must be a hundred percent sure about whether you should have spent in a particular case or not.

If you learn the art of saving more than you spend, you can easily become wealthy in a very short period. Many people understand the worth of savings. You just have to become one of them!

Use money only on an as-needed basis. If you go after your wants, I am afraid you will never be able to contain your habit of over-spending.

How much income are you saving on a daily basis? I know it's tough for a lot of us millennials to even save on a weekly or monthly basis. One of the biggest expenses that we have to deal with is that of our college. It takes tuition fees as well as our conveyance. Not to mention, there are times when we have to spend on parties and going out with friends, even when we don't want to.

Avoiding friends or your fees at your college or university isn't really possible for you. However, you can avoid certain types of expenses. For instance, you don't need any brands to survive. I know that most of you buy brands only because you are trying to impress people. That doesn't end well for anyone. Brands only make you spend more money for less value.

You can avoid buying brands any day of the week. You should get the things that you need instead of going after the things that you want. Jordan does not pay your bills, and Cindy in Versace doesn't have a clue about who you are.

Instead of spending unnecessarily on brands, you should focus on spending your money on your travels. You should not cheap out of your traveling. Instead, even if you spend a lot, you can easily get a return on investment from your travels, because the experience of traveling adds something to your resume. You have to make sure that whatever you spend brings more into your life than just a product or a service.

We only gain material things from spending on things. When we spend on traveling, we spend on our personal and spiritual development.

Through traveling, you decide to work on yourself, but there are always different ways for you to save money. For instance, if you spend because you're trying to impress other people, then you will always end up losing your hard-earned money. You must make sure that you get your money's worth.

There are individuals in my circle who can visit Dubai on less than $600. They can manage this because they have been travelling for a long time. Their prior experiences allow them to make their travels quite fruitful. Then there's me, traveling to Dubai for only $100, because I positioned myself at the right time to travel for little to nothing.

So, what would you do as an individual? If you want to succeed, how do you want to pursue the rest of your career? Do you want to stay stuck in a small office, typing away and trapped inside your own cubicle, or do you want to travel the world, and see what it's like to be out there with the real people?

You can gain more from the world than just being in one place all your life, but only experience will show you that. I can lead you down this path as your coach, and encourage you to take the first important step. However, I can't walk you down this path.

You have to make this decision on your own.

What kind of a person are you going to choose to be this year? Since you're reading this book at this very moment, it is imperative that I ask you this question.

Are you going to choose to invest in yourself, or will you just keep on incurring more expenses that you can't recover later on?

Trust me; if you spend on your travels and growing yourself, you will be able to reap much bigger benefits than just spending uselessly on things that you will consume. So, spend on your personal development, take a vacation, and go out several times a year.

Don't overthink travel!

If you've understood everything I have told you, you wouldn't have a difficult time processing the idea that I, Jasmine Branford, was able to travel to Cancun, Mexico, for less than 400 dollars.

Just say, "Wow!" I know you feel it; you just don't want to admit it!

But you will when I tell you exactly how I made this possible. This is where being smarter matters more than working harder. Even in your travels, make sure that you do smart work.

I was able to take a 7-day, all-inclusive vacation, along with hotel stays. The only reason I was able to achieve that was that I allowed myself to grow. I focused on the abilities that I had, to ensure that I got better at travel.

I chose to sow seeds to lay a firm foundation for my business. This trip was courtesy to the fact that someone offered me an opportunity to go to Mexico for a week, for only three hundred and ninety-nine dollars. That also included airfare and taxes that I had to pay along the way.

My business grew from this opportunity, and the travel became my identity from that point onwards. Why? Because I was able to save about 1000 dollars just by taking this trip for only about 400 dollars.

The amount I was able to *save* went into my business as an investment.

I have experienced the luxurious aspect of saving money and making sure that it remains as an investment for you, instead of turning into an expense that you can't quite bear.

I took a risk with traveling to Mexico, but it was because I was willing to take a risk that this travel turned my life around for the better. I spent my money on the thing that I truly believe in. Most people are afraid of investing in exactly what they believe in, because it's either too risky or seems too unreal.

People overthink when they are spending on something that doesn't give them tangible benefits. They only value tangible things that can physically provide them with something. Since people fail to see how personal development benefits them, they tend to stay away from putting money into it.

What people fail to see is that they actually become a better version of themselves, only because they choose to invest in their personal development. This is the kind of thing that you will fully understand only when you experience it yourself.

Get Paid to Travel!

At this moment, you're probably ready to find the nearest beach so that you can get away and truly start focusing on yourself. This is an amazing feeling, because now you have this burning desire that you can't get rid of.

This is a better version of you, who is now ready to live into your real purpose. What if I told you that there was a way for you to be compensated for all this travel that you want to do this year, and possibly at this very moment?

If you are going to sow seeds, and if you already have the business mindset, why not combine the two, like I did when I was 21 years old? That was when I first knew that I was going to travel, and I also knew that I wanted to see the world—but to be compensated for it as well! That was the biggest achievement of my life! That was mind-blowing for me. As a youngster, isn't that what you would do to satisfy your burning desire? Are you now ready to get up and move around to see the world? Trust me; I know exactly how you feel, because I was at the same stage in my life once too.

I suggest that you don't talk yourself out of doing these things that make you uncomfortable, because only they have the potential to get you what you want. Those are the things that you need to do in order to get to the best version of yourself!

As a millennial, you can achieve this only if you have invested the time and the effort needed to make it happen. Do you want to be a broke college student even after reading this book? Or do you want to make it big in the world? I didn't want to be the person who had to survive on cup noodles. I still wanted to be able to have options while having a full-time job and going to school full-time.

What do you want to do as a full-time millennial? Maybe you're in college. Maybe you are working a full-time job. I'm here to ask you. Are you happy in your youth? Are you truly fulfilling your purpose at the end of the day? Every millennial wants to see the world, and I'm pretty sure that they also want to be able to get paid for it.

If you're that person who doesn't want to get paid, and you want to turn down money, then this is not the book for you, because I am about to transform your life. I am here to help you grab the world by your hands. But first, you have to believe in yourself. And you have to understand that everything you do will take you to the Promised Land.

Once you start living in the land of luxury, you would never want to go back. Going broke will never be an option for you if that keeps happening.

For this, you must have a particular mindset.

Travel is now an $8 trillion industry. It is not going anywhere. When you think about travel, somehow you relate it to rich people. You relate it to celebrities or famous people who have endless resources at their disposal.

Every celebrity is moving. Every millennial is moving. Every athlete is moving. Your parents are moving. Even your classmates and teachers are moving. But what if there was a way for you to be compensated every time you move to a different place for a vacation?

Even if you have the opportunity to take a spring break, take it. It doesn't matter whether you're in school, college, or university. Surround yourself with people who love to travel. What if I told you that there was a way for you to be compensated for travel?

For that, you must understand the process that you need to follow. When you decide to take a trip, you go online, surf the web, and of course, look for the best price. If you had to look no further, what if there was a way for you to go straight to your website and be compensated for not only your travel but for helping others?

Are you that person who loves texting? Are you that person who loves being yourself? The next time you pick up your phone, ask yourself: Does this device pay me? If you're already on the internet, why not go ahead and share the link to your website, where you, too, can be compensated in this incredible industry?

When was the last time you had a family reunion? When you had this family reunion, who paid for its expenses? Were they able to curtail their expenses by actually saving on costs?

I do it every year, and the most amazing thing is that you get successful when you start changing your mindset and your habits.

A slight change in your habits can make you a millionaire from a millennial, every single year! Not because we're young, but because we're fast, and we're ready to win at an early age.

No one wants to work all the way. You can't work until you're 50. You have to be honest with yourself. Maybe you can do it until you turn 40. My goal is to keep going until I am 30.

If you are already closer to 30, that means you have no more time to waste. What time are you willing to sacrifice, knowing that you can travel the world right now?

Take a few moments to write down some takeaways as you progress to the next chapter. Don't wait too long, because Chapter 5 will get you to the next step—one more step closer to your freedom.

Chapter 5

Enjoy Your Sleep!

"Tired minds don't plan well. Sleep first, plan later."
– Walter Reisch

24/7 Pass

Can you imagine being in your twenties, making passive income? Passive income is when you're able to make income without having to be actively doing something.

Let's keep it simple. Do you really see yourself making money in your sleep? The older you get, the less stress you should have. Most retirees' stress originates from a lack of income and freedom. You see, with the tools that we use today, such as the internet, we can do just that!

This is something that we can achieve in the digital age. The first time I was able to experience passive income was when I first launched my travel business. I had started my own travel website, which ran for 24 hours while I slept comfortably in my bed. The most powerful thing about a website is that anyone in the world can have access to it. Everyone around me is traveling as we speak. People are always looking for the best deals, constantly looking for the quickest route, and living their travel experiences to the best.

When was the last time you thought about working smarter and not harder? Trust me, the older you get, the more you are going to realize that working for another human being may not be the most fun thing to do in the world. Being your own boss has its own appeal.

Making passive income can be one of the most life-changing moments in your life. For that, you have to simply put your website, your product, and the tool that you want to use, out there, so that people can see what you're doing. Transparency is the key to your business being fair. You're a millennial. Do you know how powerful it will be to grind hard in your younger days, and receive an income without you having to touch it? It's every retiree's dream. Most retirees today wish that they had made more, which is why most get another job after retirement, but that won't be in your plan. Who wants to work, after work? I sure don't! Plan to retire young so that you can enjoy your senior years with more laughs, more peace, and less stress. Follow your destiny now, with expectations of living an abundant lifestyle. The goals and disciplines you set today will play a major role in your future, and I can guarantee that the generation after you will appreciate it too.

For a few minutes, visualize your life right now. Think about how many hours in a week you spend working, hunched away at a desk, leaving yourself exhausted by the time you get home. The only time you have for leisure is over the weekends, except bosses think nothing of asking their employees to drop in for a "few minutes" on Saturday and Sunday!

Plus, this economy makes it so hard to make enough money to spend on leisure time. The weeks add up, and in the end, you're spending the majority of your years working at jobs you don't even like.

It's not even your fault. The system is simply designed that way: When you're not your own boss, you are taken advantage of.

Now, think about how different and exciting it would be if you had the time and energy to devote to yourself instead of an unfulfilling job!

A life like that is closer to being within your grasp than you might think. Your job is to provide the world with popular necessities that millennials like you and me use every day.

We live our lives out in front of screens. That's just the way the world is now, and we millennials adapted to this new way of life. The news may be filled with scare stories of how technology is taking over our lives, but the fact of the matter is that there are plenty of opportunities to benefit from these screens.

So, if we position ourselves to share a service so that it's in front of everyone's eyes, hitting the alarm clock won't be an issue anymore. As the millennial target market clicks on the service we've shared, we'll be making passive income while we're sleeping!

Isn't that something worth learning? Just think of all the time this frees up in your life!

To learn how to do this, visit MInvasion.com to set up your first coaching call. Arm yourself with the knowledge you need, not just to survive but to thrive in an online world!

Take a few moments to write down some takeaways as you progress to the next chapter. Don't wait too long, because Chapter 6 will get you to the next step—one more step closer to your freedom.

Chapter 6

Branding Is the New $uccess

*"Your brand is your name, basically.
A lot of people don't know that they need to build their brand;
your brand is what keeps you moving."*
-– Meek Mill

Your Name Can Change Your Life

From the beginning, when your name is mentioned to someone, a certain image is already being portrayed in someone's mind. When an individual hears your name, what do you think comes to their mind? Growing up, you've been taught how to behave in certain areas in your life because your legal guardian knew that your behavior would reflect on their life as well. Now that you're a young adult, everything you do in life reflects in your personality: the way you talk, walk, the way you appear in public, and so much more. You are a walking resume! Keep in mind that everyone's opinion of you will not be the same. Think of the different associations you give your time to. There's a time to be serious and a time to let your hair down, but you get to make the decisions on who gets to meet the different versions of you!

Success Story #4

The version that the public should only see is your beliefs about your success. For years, I was blessed to attend school with a young man named Richard Ragland, who had a smile that would light up the room! Every door Richard walked through, people's smiles would match his because the class clown always had a way of grabbing the attention of even the quietest person in the room.

Like everyone, we all have our ups and downs, but Richard only allowed the public to see his light shine as he lived his best life with a consistent attitude of joy, positivity, and adventure. At the age of 18, he stayed true to himself and allowed network marketing to help him put as many smiles on other individual faces around the world as he helped them believe again.

Everywhere Richard traveled, he made friends first, and eventually, business partners as well. At the age of 23, Richard passed away from this universe. He was no longer with us. Never in my life have I witnessed so many people, around the world, travel to this little town called Conyers, Georgia, to pay their respects to a young man that the majority of them had only met once!

Many people weren't even able to make it inside the church, because the lines were just as long as the ones outside the store when the newest pair of Jordans are released, which Richard loved as well.

At that very moment, I knew my friend had left his mark. I knew he had touched many souls and had changed their lives as well. To this day, many people are motivated to travel and see the world because Richard inspired them to want more, and forever will his name and success be remembered.

You stand for freedom, financial freedom, time freedom, and generational curse freedom! Now you have to create an avatar and decide what that looks like to you.

Does your freedom have a certain color? How many vacations does your freedom take in a year? What makes your millennialness different from others?

Give your liberty, goals, and philosophies a persona, and ask yourself who you want this persona to be. How does he or she look? What does this persona like to do? Does he or she like shopping and giving back to the community? Does he or she speak multiple languages? Once you zero in and get that detailed image of what you represent, you will have a certain audience that you're targeting, and that audience will now know your name. People naturally follow others who share the same beliefs and characteristics as them, but your creativity, boldness, and mindset of changing your circumstance will be just a few things that will separate you from other millennials.

The key to all of this is being consistent and true to your name, because it is your brand. Think about Will Smith, Michael Jackson, Beyoncé, and other celebrity names. They are not just A-list Hollywood celebs, but their very names hold value.

Social Media Blow Up!

There is absolutely no excuse! M.A.D. millennial, you are living in the best times, where you can simply take your brand to the next level on social media. There are two types of people in this world: one who uses the social platform to change their life, and one who just tunes into the platform to be entertained and distracted from their reality. How is life going for you right now? If you're where you want to be, and you're living out your dreams, then you have absolutely every right to spend hours online to be entertained.

People who are still trying to figure out their purpose, who want to make a better living, and want more for themselves, shouldn't spend time looking for entertainment. They need to stop running from their true destiny and, instead, use that time on gaining knowledge: the difference between the rich and the poor.

For once, turn off the TV, and open a book! The talk of early retirement is not 55 anymore; it's 30, so every second counts. In your mind, you have to believe that you have already "made it" for it to become your reality.

Facebook, Instagram, Snapchat, and many others have made it simple for you to connect with the entire world. All you have to do is promote whatever it is that you have to offer. Look at all the entertainers you watch online every day. They take a stand on entrepreneurship, putting their name on notice so that people like you can help put food on their tables as they continue to make a living doing what they love.

Social platforms allow you to be whoever you want to be, which is why you have to know who your avatar is. Every day, your job is adding value to your platform, and it must be more than once. In the world of entertainment, we see commercials constantly, and your brand should be treated in the same way.

Living life as a secret creates no wealth if no one knows who you are. So tomorrow, I challenge you to promote yourself, whether it's a photo, a video, or a live session.

Give your audience something that they can relate to, but this is your time to be creative. Become very conscious of what you post. Remember, your content can either help make you or break you. There will be days when you will want to step out of character and just post content because you may have found it amusing, and there will be days when everyone won't agree with your posts, but this is why you have to have an accountability partner. An accountability partner will be your strength on your weak days, and will make sure your brand is protected. The worst feeling is building up a platform to make a change, and seeing it destroyed within a matter of a few hours because of one post. Whatever you decide to post, stand behind it 100%, not 50%.

Of course, there will be days when you're more personal than other days, but everything is not meant for the world to see. Your idols are always living up to their brand because it is their brands that hold a lot of power when it comes down to success. If we knew everything about celebs, they probably wouldn't be as big of stars as they are today. Hold on to your audience, and find ways to grow it daily.

Once your brand becomes massive, you will be able to connect with many other audiences that can relate to what you stand for. It's not always about sprinting, but it is a marathon; so keep pressing forward, and watch how doors will start to open for you. I've witnessed followers all over social media show off their talent to the world, and within weeks, months, and years, their value in net worth increased because their brand increased. Do you believe in your beliefs? Are you truly passionate about new business ventures that will make a difference? Show the world today what you're made of, and with time, maybe in even less than four years, you will see how social media can help your contribution to the world.

Take a few moments to write down some takeaways as you progress to the next chapter. Don't wait too long, because Chapter 7 will get you to the next step—one more step closer to your freedom.

Chapter 7

Keeping Your Dream Alive

"It's not what other people believe you can do;
it's what you believe you can do."
– Gail Devers

One of the hardest things you'll do in your life is going to be learning how to keep your dream alive, and how to focus all of your energy and efforts on your goal. Dreams are the backbone of society and contribute to ambition and innovation; it is important that we never stop dreaming.

Do you think we would have gotten electricity if Nikola Tesla had sat on his butt all day long and worked a 9–5 job?

The answer is no!

We got electricity, airplanes, cars, and machinery because people like Tesla, the Wright brothers, and Karl Benz kept their dreams alive and did something amazing. And I am here to tell you that you can do the same in your life!

Not everyone is raised behind a white picket fence, and I've realized that. I've also realized that as you get older, your dreams take a backseat to your list of priorities. But that doesn't mean you should give up. This is still your life, and you can drive it in whatever direction you want to.

Can You Afford to Sleep on Your Dream?

Absolutely not!

Why?

Your dreams are like an intangible treasure that you own and that no one can steal from you. If you sleep on them, it's like sleeping on your treasure. You will not be using it according to its worth. Dreams are just that important in life.

However, in the rush of our lives, most of us end up either forgetting our biggest dreams or prioritizing them last. As a result, we end up losing anything essential that we can gain from our dreams and aspirations in life. Men and women alike face more or less similar issues when it comes to living their dreams, but I want to elaborate separately on the problems that millennial men and women face, so that others can learn to avoid them.

It took me 24 years to attend my first women's event, to hear the different challenges we women face every day; and we are not alone. Some of you have dealt with molestation, and a good number of us millennials might get pregnant at an early age. You might be trying to figure out how you are going to feed your child or look after your child. How are you going to make a living, and move on to the next step in your life, while you are struggling or a single mother?

Some young millennial women are dealing with depression at a young age because of early pregnancies and several other reasons.

Some of you struggle a lot because you don't have a guide in life to show you the way. You may not have a friend or a mother or a sister who hears your thoughts and helps you in your tough time. Or you don't feel comfortable talking about your mental health. I know there are a lot of you. There are women like that in network marketing too, but the beauty of this field is that you get to choose when you're ready to make time for your dreams. As a woman, I understand the hardships you are facing right now. I do, but that is not an excuse to give up. Watch out, and don't fall victim to that particular community of women that chooses to bash each other instead of uplifting each other.

You can always give a little more, strive a little harder, and you'll be on your path. I understand that young millennial women deal with depression a lot. I want to tell you that I have been vulnerable in my life too. I have also dealt with things. Wherever you are right now, I have been there before. I have allowed my emotions to affect me to a point where it was harming me—to some extent, even physically. I had internal depression building up so much that it harmed me in my everyday life.

I dealt with everything, and I was bad at it too. But one day, I understood that life wasn't so easy, and I stopped. I decided to live for me. I woke up and chased my dream by doing the things that made me happy until doors started to open. I wanted to get rich. I wanted to be able to bless my family and friends. I wanted to be able to tell people that yes, I make a six-figure salary! Yes, it was hard. Yes, I am a woman! Yes, I am rock-hard! I repeat this every day until it becomes my reality, and so should you.

So, I am telling other women out there, who are going through the same thing, that it is possible to live your dream. I understand that all of you must be facing a different problem, which is unique for all of you. I am here to tell you that you can do anything, even with all the problems. You can be anything you want to be, and have everything you always wanted. Learn to control your emotions on where you want to be, and recognize how that feels every day.

Over eighty percent of the women working in network marketing are making six-figure salaries because they are actually built for this; they are strong and steadfast. All I want to do is remind you that you are strong, you are smart, you are beautiful, and you are better than what you think you can become.

In network marketing, it's all you and your work ethics. Skills are nice to have, but it's about who is going to do more than the majority. It's not like a 9–5, where you must drag yourself to work every day, five days a week, to a job you don't feel like doing at all, trying to meet the company's goals instead of your own.

I know that the main concern for most women in the corporate world is of equal pay. There's probably a guy named Sam who's getting paid more than you while he does exactly the same work that you do, and it makes your blood boil.

In network marketing, it is not about male or female; it's all about just doing the type of work you're passionate about, and earning the amount you deserve. As I said before, it's all you. You can get whatever outcome you want from it. Network marketing allows you, as a consumer, to become a retailer—and quite frankly, your own boss!

When you position yourself around the same strength, you will begin to think differently about yourself. You will see that you're as qualified as anyone else in network marketing, because this industry is filled with single and married mothers, with women dealing with depression, with people that are doing everything by themselves, and with people who think they are not living their best lives but want to change some things in their life and want a better future. Every single woman in this business, who is making six figures right now, has a story. Many have dealt with troubled pasts, and that is what made them hungrier and made them strive for more. Now it's just time to hear yours.

Let's address the men in our society now, and the problems that keep them from following their dreams.

Society has always challenged men to be the best that they can be. It has always pressured them to be leaders and to look after their families. According to societal stereotypes, men cannot be dependent on anyone; they are expected to be able to fend for themselves and lead their families and their teams.

I can tell you how network marketing will prepare you for just that. It will make you a good leader because of the self-development you will experience in this area of your career. You will understand yourself better, and your strengths and your weaknesses. You will see what makes people crack, and it will allow you to have a confidence boost. When no one is telling you anything, and you are your own boss, you won't have any room for mistakes.

Likewise, in life, no one will tell you how you should dress, sit, or work. You will feel the leadership coursing through your veins if you really have that potential in you.

Everyone is their own leader and does their work how they like.

Network marketing will allow you, as a man, to look after your family and provide them with what they need, the way you were told to do from the start. And as a millennial, it becomes harder and harder to make money and provide for your family. One source of income is just not enough.

This industry will also allow you to take time out for your family and for your job as well. Because in network marketing, you get to dictate your time; you get to dictate your future. It will provide you with greater opportunities and a better way of being independent of anything and anyone.

You cannot sleep on your dreams. You will regret it when you are 50 years old, going through your life miserably, and asking, "What if?" This "what if" is what kills people. It is what throws them inside the pit of depression. So, turn your "what if" into "I did!" The *future you* depends on you!

Dreams to Reality

How many times have you thought about your dreams and ambitions? Once a week, twice a week, every day? And how many times have you done something to get closer to your dream? Let me take a wild guess: Never, right?

It is important to think about your dreams; it's one way of visualizing what you want in life. It is what makes us human, having dreams and ambitions. But only thinking about your goals, and wishing and wanting them, won't do anything. You have to get up and work toward it physically. It won't only allow you to achieve what you always wanted to, but it will give you a sense of pride and purpose in yourself that you never had.

I know a lot of you don't even know where to start, and that is why I am here to tell you what you can do, and what you should do, to take your dream and turn it into something tangible.

Start with the End

The first step to turning your dream into a reality is to close your eyes and think about your dream.

Turn it into reality in your head first, and then look at yourself at the end. Look at yourself and what it would be like after you have achieved what you wanted to achieve. Meditate on your dream, a year or two down the line. That thought and the scene you just created in your head should become the learning power of your goals.

I want millennials to know that whatever you dream about is never too small. Whatever your dream is, it is worth it. Never dream small—hell, dreams are free, right? It doesn't take anything for you to dream. So why dream for that small sedan? Why not dream for that big Mercedes?

Why dream of a 2-bedroom house? Dream of a 6-bedroom house. Don't dream small; dream as big as you can. Never limit yourself—it's your life, and you need to be in control of it.

Believe That It Is Possible

How many people do you see, living the lifestyle that you always desire? A lot, right? So, let me tell you this: If they can do it, so can you! Never sit around, saying, "Oh, it's not possible."

Everything is possible in life. The people living luxury lifestyles are the definitive proof that it's possible.

Some people out there are doing what you love to do, and they want to learn how to do all of it. So why not pick up their habits, and pick up everything positive that they do, and everything they did to achieve what they have already achieved. I am sure you have read articles and watched videos titled, "5 Things All Successful People Do," or "10 Things CEOs Advise on Doing," or have at least read, *The 7 Habits of Highly Effective People.* Why do these articles, books, and videos exist, and why do these get so much attention?

Simply by doing what they did, and by following the advice of successful CEOs or owners of big companies, you can come closer to achieving your own dreams. This will give you an opportunity to do things ten times better, as you will learn from their mistakes and from their successes. It is important to believe in yourself and to trust yourself that you can achieve whatever it is that you want to achieve.

Share Your Dreams

Don't be afraid to tell your dreams to others. Don't keep it cooped up inside you. Leaders are vocal and are not afraid to express themselves, or to express what they think about. When you tell people about your goals and ambitions, your chances of actually following through with your dreams increase.

Confirm your affirmation, because you have witnesses. Be vocal, be proud, and have the energy to go through with it. There is nothing wrong with you sharing your dreams with other people who are as ambitious as you are, and who are as motivated as you are to make a difference in your life. Remember, whatever God has for you is simply for you! This is all a question of faith and you applying the work to match.

Surround Yourself with Supporters

No one can be motivated and work if they are surrounded by negative people who lack the same beliefs as you. These people will only drag you down. They will always make you see the negative side of your goals; they will tell you how hard it is and how it is a waste of time. Don't listen to them. Surround yourself with people who support you with their words and presence, and who tell you that yes, you can do it; you can achieve it! Surround yourself with like-minded individuals. As Oprah Winfrey said, *"Surround yourself with only people who are going to lift you higher."*

It is much easier to achieve your goals when someone gives you a little motivation, so build your support system. Look at all the greats in the world. Michael Phelps, the most decorated Olympic athlete, always had people supporting him.

Do you think Michael Phelps would have won 28 medals, 23 of them gold, if he had people bringing him down?

Of course not. Stay close to people that will only lift you and make you feel like all of your dreams are possible.

Pull the Trigger

Now it's time to put all that thinking and all that dreaming into effect. It's time to grab a piece of paper and write down your dreams, and make a step-by-step list of what needs to be done. Think thoroughly, and do your research. It is essential for you to make your dreams tangible. Grab that piece of paper, grab a pen, and write it all down.

After you have written it down, you will know what steps you have to take. Now it's time for you to pull the trigger and jump on it. Do what needs to be done. Facebook, Amazon, and Apple—all of these top companies were started in garages and dorm rooms: small spaces where Mark Zuckerberg, Jeff Bezos, and Steve Jobs pulled the triggers. They just did what was needed to be done and didn't make excuses. Look at what happened to them: All of them became billionaires.

Also, you just have to leap for it and believe in yourself that you will make it big, that you will succeed.

Have Fun

The last step in turning your dreams into reality is to have fun with the process. You are creating and making something you always dreamt of, and you should have the most fun you can have while building it.

There is no point in trying to create a future if you are going to be miserable every day. Have fun when it comes to living out your dreams. When you are writing it down on a piece of paper and planning it all out, you should be having fun doing all that. Do whatever you have to do to get excited about achieving your dreams.

Do whatever you feel like doing. It is your dream, your goal, and your ambition, and if you are not going to have fun while planning for it, and while achieving it, then who will?

Who Exactly Are You Doing This For?

I am asking you who you are doing this for. Who comes to mind when you think, "Oh, I am doing this for them?" For example, I'll ask the single and married mothers who they are doing this for. Is it for your children so that you can give them a better life? Or are you doing this for your parents? Tell yourself who you are doing this for. Of course, you are doing this for yourself, but who else? When you find that "who else" that you are doing this for, then you will be able to feel better motivated, and you will see your goals clearer than ever.

I am asking the same question to men too. Ask yourself who you are doing all of this for: Is it your children, is it your wife, or is it your parents? Find that "who," and see yourself fighting tooth and nail to achieve it.

Why? Find Your Reason

Let's face it; you need a reason to motivate yourself to follow your dreams. And life may have given you many reasons, but you just didn't see them. You have to sit down and ask yourself, why? Why do you want to change your life? Why do you want to be successful? Go deep inside yourself. Go into the deepest and darkest part of yourself, and find the "why."

Ask yourself why. Some of you might answer this question by saying, "Oh, I want to break my family's curse." Well, why do you want to break your family's curse? Is it because when you would go to the store as a kid, and you would want something, and your mom was not able to get it for you because she didn't have any money? Ask yourself why she didn't have the money to get you something that you wanted.

Maybe it's because she didn't have a good job. Ask yourself why she didn't have a good job. It was probably because she wasn't that educated. I want you to dig deep inside and go seven layers deep into the "why," and find out the main cause of your journey.

A lot of people ask themselves about their "why," at least once in their lives, and when they find it, they stick to that reason. Millennials have done this exercise before, where they have asked themselves why they are following the path they are following, and the real reason for their actions. Most people come up with an event that took place when they were very little. For several people, it is a traumatizing experience or something that they wanted to forget.

Your "why" should make you cry; it should enable you to go back in time. But also think about recent reasons, and don't stick to one reason. Maybe your girlfriend left you because you were not making enough money. Maybe your boyfriend left you because he thought you were lazy. Maybe you met your middle school bully, and they are doing better than you. Ask yourself why you are going to do what you are going to do, and I guarantee you that this will help you in achieving your goals and ambitions. Visit MInvasion.com to complete the "why" exercise today!

Now I want you to take down all of the "whys"—all 7 layers of them. I want you to think about them, and I want you to look at the last layer, the layer that made you feel like doing something about your life. Look at this last "why" every day, because that should be the reason you shouldn't give up.

M.A.D. millennial, you're ready for Chapter 8!

Chapter 8

Plan A, Plan B, Plan C

"The world changed from having the determinism of a clock to having the contingency of a pinball machine."
– Heinz R. Pagels

You never really know what's going to happen the next second. True, that shouldn't deter you from your plans, but that should certainly compel you into creating contingencies should your initial plans fail.

That's exactly what millennials need to understand. Not everyone is cut out to be an entrepreneur, or wants to be one. I know that you might want to earn money and not want to worry about logistics, hiring, or any other thing that goes into running a business.

But despite all the hassle of running your own business, its benefits are much higher. I would still encourage millennials to have multiple sources of income rather than fixating on their day job. Your additional source should be a private business that has the capacity to give you seamless benefits.

Why?

Because you don't put all of your eggs in one basket when it comes to business. Having only one source of income will make you too dependent on your job, and you wouldn't want that in the long run if you want to chase your dreams and do something big in your life.

Imagine that after years of working a 9 to 5 job, you finally decide to go after some of the dreams that you had been avoiding for a while now. It's always one thing or another that you have to do to get by; that may be because you placed your dreams in the backseat of life. Whatever savings you make, get depleted sooner or later. Eventually, you don't have the money you need to fulfill any of the dreams you had planned.

You need to have another source of income, only so that you can spend on your dreams along with saving for a secure future.

Imagine another situation in which you have two sources of income available. In this scenario, your savings won't run out because your other sources of income would be adding to them constantly. In this case, you won't have to stop in the middle and look for work again, and put your dreams on hold yet again. Being able to fulfill your dreams is just one of the reasons for you to have a second income. If the last decade has taught us anything, it's that no job is safe anymore. Job security and contracts are a thing of the past.

The economy is like a river that can be sped up by a little rain one day, and be slower than a turtle the day after. Therefore, it's best to have multiple streams of income if you don't want to drown in a flood. Unfortunately, a lot of people only stick to their day job as their primary source of income, which can cause a lot of problems for them due to a host of different reasons.

People still look at these day jobs as their main source of income. Many millennials face trouble working in their 9 to 5 jobs, whether it is due to a lack of experience or not wanting to work in a boring job, but they have to meet their expenses. It leads to depression and the feeling of being stuck, which only makes one hate their life. But it doesn't need to be this way for you too. All of this can change if only you decide to look for other sources of income, ones that involve your passion. I know you are not completely sold on my point, so let me give you four reasons that showcase the importance of having a second source of income.

Job Security

You get up early in the morning, at around 7:00 am, so that you can get to work by 9:00 am sharp. You try to be as punctual and regular in your 9 to 5 job as possible. Traditionally, your day job needs that kind of attention.

You try your best to climb up the corporate ladder and stay there long enough to retire with a handsome salary and a huge retirement benefit. However, with the emergence of e-commerce, companies that were considered safe for several years, have been going out of business and have been forced to make the necessary layoffs.

Look at Amazon and how it has changed the landscape of shopping for millions around the globe. The massive success that Amazon has received has affected its competitors in the worst possible way. Places like Best Buy and Nordstrom have announced layoffs because Amazon is beating them down with tough competition.

Steam and other game selling websites have left Game Stop deserted.

While some might see this boom of the internet as adversity, I want you to view this as an opportunity. The internet has made it possible for you to make a living for yourself, even when you work from the comfort of your home.

There are many possibilities out there for you. You can open up an online business in any industry because of the diversity of opportunities extended by the internet.

The start-up cost is extremely low, as you don't need a place of business when you're starting. You can tap into a variety of markets, which ultimately leads you to network marketing for your business.

As a millennial, you have little time to yourself as it is, and it is a difficult job to invest that time into coming up with an idea for a product, finding manufacturers for it, and finally putting them up on your website for sale, which is a difficult job. You will have to compromise on your personal time to start a business after work hours.

Network marketing or multi-level marketing is the best thing for millennials who take their "me" time seriously.

Moral Environment

When you need something desperately, you barely stop to think about the consequences of the things that you do to get to that particular thing. Many of us have been through this. In the fast-paced world of today, millennials have to deal with several instances where they compromise their work ethic to satisfy their bosses or managers.

In a full-time job, you don't have a choice but to put up with some of the unethical or illegal activities that the business you work for indulges in. However, as a business owner, you can make sure that none of your moral values have to be compromised in your own business dealings.

Inclination for Taking Risks

In a job, you are safe from risk since you are not the one making any decisions. In contrast to that, when you start your business, you have to take risks. Your investment and your time are both at risk when you start your business. You may fail abruptly and lose everything you have at stake.

However, if you opt for network marketing of your business, you have an opportunity to protect yourself from unnecessary risk.

At this stage in your life, as a young individual, you can take this type of risk and still survive with it. When you're in your middle age, with children and responsibilities to take care of, you tend not to go for a business that might risk your livelihood.

Now is the right time for you to take the risk of starting something that holds the potential to challenge your financial stability.

Paying Off Debts with Ease

Sadly, millennials are graduating with more debts than any other generation. Having multiple employments will help you pay off your debts. You will be able to pay off a large chunk of your liabilities when you make a huge income at the end of each month.

Finding a second employment option that pays well and still allows you to focus on yourself is hard, and that's why I am going to recommend to you the option of network marketing. It is fast and reliable, and allows you to get a good amount of money for less work than conventional jobs.

Are You Working to Live? Or Living to Work?

What's the basic difference?

We all find jobs and sources of income because we have to find our means of living. No one can survive without making money. However, some people work so much that it seems as if they are alive only to work.

Very few people can ensure that their work stays a part of their life instead of becoming the whole of it.

Let's understand the difference between the two, in detail.

Live to Work

Basically, for a person who lives to work, their entire life revolves around their work. Their work is their foremost priority in life. Everything else comes after it.

Most people live their lives in this way because, by competing with their colleagues, they find a form of self-satisfaction that isn't available elsewhere. They end up focusing all of their energy into their work, whether they are paid highly for it or not.

Work to Live

This is the ideal way of life. People who lead this life understand that work is only necessary to support themselves and their dependents financially. Their interests lie in other places, and their work is just a duty that they have to fulfill to get by.

These people try to get maximum pay for minimum effort. They take pride in their jobs, and they try to perform their best. However, their work is not their only priority.

It is important to detect and seek out whether you are living to work or working to live. It will allow you to set down realistic expectations for yourself, and to choose the correct career path.

Some people may have little interest in their current employment because they're not getting paid well for it. Some may find it boring because they don't enjoy their core responsibilities.

Others may feel absolutely comfortable in their jobs because they put it before everything else in their lives.

Network marketing allows you to create a work-life balance that gives you time for your personal life just as much as your professional life.

In this field, you can work from home, where you assign yourself working hours that keep you comfortable. It is the best choice for you if you have a hard life at home.

However, nothing comes easily. You may not feel very confident about owning your business. You may need appropriate guidance.

How about mentorship?

Mentorships

If Oprah Winfrey and Michael Jordan can have mentors, then I am sure you can too.

Don't be afraid of observing and asking for help from people older than you, or people who have more experience than you. Most of the time, people won't mind you asking for help, so don't hesitate to reach out to the people that you consider experts in your line of work.

That's how you find mentors that can help you set your feet firmly in whatever field you choose.

There's a famous quote attributed to both Benjamin Franklin and Confucius, *"Tell me and I forget; teach me and I may remember; involve me and I learn."*

Mentors have the ability to involve you while they teach you how to do your best. I have met many newcomers in network marketing who are quite shaky when it comes to making a sound decision about a particular issue. I have been a mentor to many people, and I know that they need someone they trust and respect to show them the way forward in their path.

When you are looking for a mentor, make sure that you share a healthy, trust-based relationship with them.

Oprah Winfrey stated, *"A mentor is someone who allows you to see the hope inside yourself."*

Mentors are there no matter what; they provide moral support and cheer you on. They won't let you stop, and they will always push you one step further to your goal.

Mentors can be connectors as well. They can perform a dual role. The first is of helping you in your journey with knowledge and encouragement. The second is using their connections to help you succeed and achieve your end goal. Most mentors have a lot of connections in the industry they are in, and they will gladly connect you with people who are willing to work with you.

In order to let a mentor help you, you must have an attitude that is open to learning. Many millennials have a know-it-all attitude that can prove to be quite damning for them. Basically, this kind of thinking limits our learning potential. When we don't think we need to improve, we never take the advice of someone who has more experience than us.

People who have this *"I don't agree"* attitude, shun anyone and everyone who contradicts them or tries to tell them to improve. They always think that they are right, and they can never be wrong.

If you are one of these people, then you need to change. You need to be coachable and become an information sponge. Just soak in as much information as you can, from anywhere you can get it. Make sure never to stop learning, because by learning, you are able to grow, and if you grow, you will succeed. Have an open mind, be open to learning, and set goals. I cannot stress it enough how important it is for you to set your goals and plan everything out before you jump into network marketing.

Setting Goals

Goal setting should be taken seriously as a wholly separate task in your life. People over-estimate their abilities and set big goals that they keep chasing and never end up achieving.

For instance, becoming the CEO of a multi-national company is a big, long-term goal. You will have to work for a few more years on achieving this goal. However, getting a job is a small goal that can be attained in the near future.

When you're setting your goals, you should make sure that you have a few small goals along with the big ones, so that you don't feel demotivated from always running behind the big ones. A little bit of achievement, no matter how small, can prove to be a huge motivator.

In fact, you can even set a series of small goals that lead you to your final, big goal.

For instance, you begin with goal number one.

Goal one is to get employed. Once you get employed, you immediately get a sense of satisfaction that you have accomplished this goal in your life.

Goal two is to get your first promotion. When you get a promotion, you feel a sense of attainment. Getting a win one more time makes you more confident in life. Now you can move on to your next goal.

Goal three is to get into a leading position in your team. After a year and a half at your job, you finally become a team lead. Again, this achievement will motivate you to keep going until you finally have achieved all of your goals, and have made it to the big one in the end.

This will help you stay focused and will allow you to relax from time to time, which is really necessary for the longevity of your motivation. This small goal setting will allow you to measure the progress you have made throughout the years, and it will reflect positively on your overall personality. Small goals will limit the procrastination we are all prone to. One big goal might have you slacking from time to time, but with small goals, you will have little time to achieve them, so you won't have enough time to waste. You can start these goals as early as possible.

Give yourself deadlines so that you don't procrastinate, and so that you have the motivation to follow through on your goals.

Your goals must be specific, measurable, achievable, relevant, and time-bound—or **S.M.A.R.T.** for short—for them to be truly motivating.

SMART is a tool that is used in project management all the time, so if organizations use it in their project management, then I think you can use it your own life as well.

Stay motivated, and stay ahead of others!

M.A.D. millennial, you're ready for Chapter 9!

Chapter 9

Take Back Control!

"You just try to figure out ways to slow the game down to get back to the pace that you want it to be at, to try to get the momentum back on your side."
– Matt Cain

Millennials, ask yourself this: "Do I have what I deserve?"

Ask yourself this—not once, not twice, but multiple times in a day!

You need to believe that you don't have everything you deserve in life, and that you can always do better. Believe in yourself. Believe that you will make it work and that you will get whatever you want. You need to have a can-do attitude for your dreams to turn into reality. I want you to dig deep within yourself and realize your worth. Only then will you be able to give yourself all that you dream of. You need to give yourself your inheritance!

Get Your Inheritance

What do I mean by "get your inheritance?"

I don't mean that you need to go ask your parents for your inheritance in the family property. No, that will come to you in due time. I want you to define your worth and give yourself everything that has been your right since birth. You need to get what you deserve, and you can only do that when you have full confidence in yourself.

You are unique, and you should never compare yourself to anyone. Everyone is the best in their own capacity. You have to understand that. Don't be overwhelmed by anyone else's speed of achieving great things in life. Your time will come too.

Always value yourself at the highest level. Stop comparing yourself to others, and start living.

You can use network marketing to get your inheritance. You were not born to live in poverty. You deserve as much wealth as you can accumulate. Once you have that clarified in your own mind, you will be able to create your reality in the exact same way!

The best part about using network marketing is that you get to help others in achieving their dreams and ambitions while you work on yours. In network marketing, you have to seek people, and you have to help them achieve their dreams. This is what I have always appreciated about this industry. It is more about "us" and less about "me."

The amazing thing about the "us" approach is that it is an inclusive approach, and that's what network marketing is all about!

When you are looking to get your inheritance, you must contemplate the question: Are you willing to help?

Once you understand how you can achieve your dream, you have to help others in doing the same thing.

You can help others by sharing your knowledge of the skills you have developed, no matter what skill it is. Sharing will multiply your efforts and will yield you better results.

Be a leader. Seek people who need help, and guide them with your knowledge so that they are in a better position to attain their goal. Think of yourself as a tree whose fruit is knowledge.

You can share this knowledge with others. Sharing will make you feel content with yourself and will allow you to discover who you are— the next step in taking control of your life. You can only do that by getting to know who you are.

You have to ask yourself who you want to be in life. Do you want to be a leader or a follower? Do you want to be a lender or a borrower? Do you want to keep taking from your community, or do you finally want to start giving back? Find out exactly who you are!

Who Are You?

No one knows who they are until they set out on the path to discover themselves.

First, you need to define what your personality is like. Do you like to lead or to follow? You need to define yourself before you can start helping others.

What is your passion? Once you get a clearer vision of who you are, life becomes simpler. Learn to live life with intention, attention, and no tension.

If you want to be a leader instead of a follower, tell yourself that you are a leader every day, and act accordingly. A leader sets an example for their sub-ordinates to follow. They help others in achieving their goals, and they tell people exactly what needs to be done!

If you want to be a lender now, instead of being the borrower, then you have to believe that you can get in this position, before it happens to you. If you want to give back to the community instead of taking from it, then tell yourself that you have more than enough to give away, and you will become just that. Give back, donate, spread knowledge, and help others with their problems.

You need to find yourself before you can step forward and achieve the next step in becoming successful through network marketing. I am going to discuss with you a few techniques you can use to find yourself and be close to your mind, body, and soul.

Know Your Core Values

Core values are the morals and principles you hold near and dear to your heart. You may learn these values through your parents. These values define you for the most part.

Your core values play a significant role in the decisions you make on a daily basis. They reflect in the way you communicate with others and how you deal with conflict. At home, at work, or out with friends, the values that you cannot compromise on are your core values and the building blocks of your character. Your core values could be any or all of honesty, dedication, flexibility, wisdom, or passion for learning.

They define you. Once you start living by them, you must own them. You should never surrender them for anything. Only then can you develop a strong image for yourself, in front of those who care about you and hope to see you succeed.

Know What You Like and Don't Like

Being aware of your likes and dislikes gives you a better understanding of your own personality. You become confident because you now know exactly what you want and don't want. By this, you can be your own person, and you can ditch the whole act of doing what is popular and avoiding what's not cool. In this way, you just focus on the task at hand, and give your all into making it a success.

Although there is nothing wrong with doing what is popular, if you are only doing it because of its popularity, you are not focusing on the value of the task.

Take some time out to define what you like or dislike, and put yourself in charge of making this decision, not your family and friends. Stay true to your likes and dislikes—no one else has to like them but you.

Sometimes you do things because the people who care about you think that they are beneficial for you. When you do that, your heart's not in it. You do them to keep your loved ones happy.

This even applies to you saying yes when you should have said no. At times, you even agree to attend parties that you don't want to attend. It might seem impolite sometimes to voice that you don't want to go to another party this week. But if you keep thinking that it might be impolite, and continue to do things that frustrate you, this will only lead you to being unhappy, and you will lose a part of yourself. It takes guts to define what you don't like. And even more to stick with them.

Know Your Dream

Your dreams and hopes are the things that will shape your future, because that is what you wish and look forward to accomplishing, and you take constant strides for fulfilling them.

From the beginning of this book, I have been emphasizing the importance of dreaming and knowing what you want in life.

Your dreams are like the objective that you wish to attain in life. When you have your dream in perspective, you know what you're aiming for. You need to have the destination in view and mind before you can start your journey.

Knowing what you want in life is a great describing factor for you, your personality, and your character. Learn to understand the details and specifics of your dream. Make your dream a part of your daily pursuit, and take it seriously, because if you won't, no one else will.

Push forward to live a life with a natural high, a life that keeps you on cloud 9, 24/7—and you don't need to take any substance or drug to take you there.

Be high on life, enjoy waking up every day, and live your best life chasing your dreams and achieving something big. This is the way you will truly know who you actually are.

Regardless of whether you are finding yourself or trying to achieve your life's goal, trusting and not losing your sight is the most important thing you can do. That is why, after finding yourself, you need to believe and have faith in the journey you have embarked on.

Trust the Process

You can become a little frustrated when you don't see yourself achieving what you want quickly. However, you shouldn't lose hope so soon. Believe in the term, *"Trust the process."*

This term was coined by Sam Hinkie, a former general manager of the Philadelphia 76ers. It was his strategy that kept him trusting the process he followed or was made to follow.

He used this strategy for acquiring draft picks, a young player, and players with trade-friendly contracts, to bring in a superstar player.[1]

Now, when Sam Hinkie said to trust the process, he meant that it would take time to achieve your goal, but it is important to not lose motivation, and to keep your faith in the process designed, in any case.

In your life, you sometimes become restless when you don't see results materializing soon. As a consequence, you doubt everything that happens to you. Everything happens in its own time. You just have to trust that the process you are following will pay off one day. You have to keep in mind that success will not come to you overnight; there will be countless hours of hard work and dedication behind it. You have to enlist your trust in the step-by-step process that you are going through. In order to achieve that big goal, you have to learn to wait. Waiting comes with being rooted and remaining still in the same soil you first planted your seeds in. I get it! We're millennials! We get distracted, and we're always ready for the next big thing. Think about it; if every tree you see today kept jumping from soil to soil, could it grow to its fullest potential? No, a strong tree has to have strong roots, and in order to get strong roots, it has to remain in the same soil. So, my millennial friend, don't rush this process and learn to BE STILL! Your time will come.

Your journey to the end goal will not be without hard work and trials. If you get disappointed at every step of the way, you will never be successful in life.

There is a process for everything in life. There's a process for graduating, and there's one for getting a job, and there's another one

1

[1] Khadrice Rollins. (2018). What does 'Trust the Process' mean? Retrieved from: https://www.si.com/nba/2018/trust-the-process-meaning-philadelphia-76ers-team-motto

for getting married or moving to another country! Nothing happens in the world without a process. The sooner you start trusting the process, you will be able to achieve your dreams just as soon.

The universe is not going to change its rules for you. When there is a process for everything else in life, there will always be one for achieving success too.

Much like how you have to dribble a ball down the court in order to shoot a basket, or how you have to run down the field in order to get that touchdown, staying motivated is a tough thing. That's why I have discussed goal setting in the previous chapters. Set little goals so that you can stay motivated in the long run by achieving them one by one as you go on.

What do you do after you have been through the process and have achieved all that you wanted to achieve?

Let me tell you this: The process is not over. In the previous chapters, I talked about sharing information and becoming a leader and a mentor. Well, this is where the process really starts. After you have gotten to your desired destination, you should help others in getting to theirs.

This is where all your hard work pays off. When you are able to influence people positively, helping them get to where they need to be, you will feel quite satisfied with yourself. To some extent, you will love the way you have become successful in your life, and how you're helping others do the same thing.

You have to make up your mind to help people and become a mentor after you have achieved something in life. When you see yourself in their shoes, you can understand their problems. As a millennial, you have the tools to help them do much better!

You can use network marketing to achieve not only your goal but the goals of people who look up to you. You can go out and help people by giving them a step-by-step guide so that they can understand the ins and outs of network marketing. The way you have created success for yourself, you can help others do the same thing.

If cold reactions and negative remarks meet you, don't feel disheartened; they are not meant to make you feel bad for trying to help them. You should understand that not all people would want a step-by-step guide, so you would have to let go of the hands of some people, but don't let this cloud your judgment and make you bitter.

Remember, when you choose to be a leader or a lender, or someone who is at a higher position than others, you decide your own fate. In such a case, you put yourself in a giving position. You can give by sharing the information that you have acquired after hours and hours of grinding and moving successfully with everyone.

Be a true leader and put the information out there. Then let the people use the fruits of your labor. You must have the emotion of sacrifice alive inside you to be able to achieve great success in life.

Don't let the people who refuse to accept your help bring you down. Don't focus on the number of no's that you have to hear from people.

Even if you help just one person, that satisfaction will trump any and all of the no's or rude comments you have to face. You need to have the courage to let people know that it doesn't bother you if they turn you down.

You need to keep your integrity intact and take everything head on like the champion you are!

Remaining Excited

Your dream is quite far from you today. In order to get to that, you have to stay motivated for a long time. The only way you can do that is by remaining excited for as long as it's possible.

Listen to something motivating every single day. Don't let any sort of negativity fill your head. Add energy to each and everything that you do.

True, I have mentioned a few times that you should do the things that you want to do. However, you can't always achieve the lifestyle that you desire by only doing the things that you want. Sometimes you have to do things you don't enjoy doing. In this scenario, your compulsion might reduce the quality of the work you're doing.

In order to curtail that, you must add energy to each and everything that you do, so that it retains the quality it should have, and becomes something that you enjoy to the best of your ability!

While you enjoy the process of getting there, you won't even notice when you have made it to the finish line and have attained the goal you had set for yourself.

During this process, the toughest thing is to wake up just as excited on the 500th day as you did on the 1st day. There are a lot of ways that you can use to maintain your excitement. I have already discussed a few of those in the previous chapters. If you have forgotten about them, you can go through them again to get updated. I will mention a few ways here as well, and tell you the importance of remaining excited.

You need to stay motivated and wake up after a year just as excited as you were on the first day of the year. To stay motivated, you have to celebrate every win that comes your way.

No matter how small, celebrate every tiny target that you have achieved. Treat yourself often with your favorite cake or anything else that excites you. The bigger the goal you have achieved, the bigger the celebration should be. Celebrate with anything that makes you genuinely happy.

While doing this, you must stay away from negativity at all costs. Avoid listening to and seeing things that make you feel bad. Whatever you listen to and see in your surroundings, becomes a part of your belief system. When you avoid experiencing negative things, you keep your belief system from getting tainted with negativity.

Another way you can stay motivated and excited is by having complete trust in yourself. Let's face it; you lose trust in yourself faster than you lose trust in an unfaithful partner. So it is important to trust yourself soon. You have to constantly tell yourself that you will achieve every single thing in your mind, and you will suffice.

The reason I keep mentioning motivation and being excited is that it is the toughest thing to feel when you have gone well into your goal, but you are not seeing results as rapidly as you thought.

The thing is, people chase their dreams, but from day one, they think that they'll have this in a hundred days and they'll have that in 200 days. So when they fall a little behind on their plans, they get demotivated. Most of the time, people ignore the fact that they were planning out and setting their goals for something tough, which may even be unachievable to many others.

To endure this tough journey, you have to stay excited throughout it. You can learn persistence and consistency from professional athletes. Not all athletes get to win the championship in a year, but they don't give up when they don't win; they come back stronger and try even harder. If they can do it, so can you! No matter what your goal is—whether it is to get that championship or make a million dollars—you need persistence, consistency, dedication, and excitement to make it all happen!

You may or may not have heard this before, but you become what you hear and see. You watch motivational videos, and you feel motivated; you listen to sad songs, and you get sad. It happens, and the effect is strong, so you need to control what you hear and see.

Get in Control of What You See and Hear

Your parents had influence over you when you were a child. Your friends had it over you when you were a teenager. I am pretty sure that even as a millennial, many people have influence over you, and you have influenced quite a few people yourself.

Influence is the one thing that you will always have in your life. That's why you should listen to podcasts that motivate you in your everyday life and keep you energized. Listen to them in the morning or during the time you are driving to work. In this way, you won't have to make extra hours in your day to give to them, and you will have a pleasant ride to work.

You can watch inspiring TED talks and motivational videos in your spare time. You can use anything that floats your boat. It is vital to have a visual and auditory stimulation of motivation for your mind.

You need to be careful with this because this is what builds your belief system. You need to stay away from negativity. Just like videos and audios are motivating or demotivating, there are people who will either motivate you or demotivate you. You need to cut the deadweight of the negative people from your life, and give your time and attention to the positive people who can bring out the best in you!

Avoid the Nay-Sayers

You will meet many people in your life who will tell you that what you are doing is too hard, and that it will take way too much time and effort. Don't ever listen to them, because all they will try to do is bring you down.

Don't let people steer you away from your dreams. A lot of times, people will tell you that your dream is too hard, and that you should follow their advice and do what they are telling you. You simply cannot let them deviate you from your path; your dream is achievable and manageable, and you need to believe in that!

You need to be selfish, and you need to tell them NO! You need to think about yourself. It is okay to be selfish, and it is okay to lose some people down the line. Lose the deadweight.

I promise you, the people who are actually with you to support you and believe in you will never get left behind. Think of this year as YOUR year. This is your year to get closer to your dream. It's your year to create the new circle of people around you that will support you in your journey. It's your year to be selfish and live a little for yourself.

Think of yourself as a rocket ship blasting off. You are not going to land. You have taken off, and you are just going to keep on going and going and going—you won't stop until you enter the new space. Remain motivated, and always stay excited and have fun on your journey!

M.A.D. Millennial, you're ready for Chapter 10!

Chapter 10

Get Ready to Take Off!

"Millennials have grown up with technology,
and they're used to having their voices heard."
– Joe Wiggins, Head of Communications at Glassdoor

As a network marketer, you need to wholeheartedly believe in this quote by Joe Wiggins, because this is the exact essence of it. As a millennial, you always have your phone with you, and you are always browsing social media. You share your experiences with everyone that follows you. Whether you go to an amusement park or a funeral, you tell the world how it went and how it felt like being there.

Millennials are used to having their voices heard because of Twitter, Facebook, and other social networking sites. You can easily share your thoughts and opinions over the internet on different issues, whether they are about serious matters or just about pop culture. This easy communication through widespread platforms for sharing has given millennials a unique skill that baby boomers never possessed—that of effective communication.

There are a lot of baby boomers who are amazing at sales and marketing. But let's face it; the world we are living in right now needs fresh minds with fresh ideas. That is where millennials—you—come in. You are ripe for network marketing. There are a host of reasons that millennials are so successful in network marketing. Let's discuss some of the reasons in this chapter.

Millennials – Best Suited for Network Marketing

Millennials are changing the fields of sales and marketing. They are shifting the landscape of marketing in two ways: by being challenging consumers, and by being innovative marketers and sales reps. Millennials are the largest cohort demographically after baby boomers, with a population of over 80 million.[2] With the sheer size and technological advancement of the recent decade, millennials have become a powerhouse of groundbreaking techniques. They have a better understanding of the demographics because of the knowledge they are given access to. Honestly, the majority of the people who are willing to spend on new projects in the market are millennials. Generation Y is not only the most entrepreneurial generation, but they are smarter than many generations before it. They are at an advantage because they have information available to them at their fingertips. They are financially smarter when compared with the previous generations.[3]

Seeing how they are better suited to sell to other millennials, they are the prime people that do well in network marketing. The following are the reasons that network marketing is a prosperous option for millennials.

[2] Sassy Suite. (2015). How to connect millennials with direct sales and network marketing. Retrieved from: https://www.sassysuite.com/how-to-connect-millennials-with-direct-sales-and-network-marketing/

[3] Richie Norton. (2017). The 14 most destructive millennial myths debunked by Data. Retrieved from: https://medium.com/the-mission/the-14-most-destructive-millennial-myths-debunked-by-data-aa00838eecd6

Millennials Know Millennials

Millennials think, act, and process information differently than previous generations. It is because of the exposure they have received. There are more millennial buyers in the market than any other generation, which ultimately means that companies require millennials to sell their products.

Millennials Are Changing How Sales Works

Millennials have had an impact on each and everything we do currently, and it is just a matter of time before they take sales and marketing to the next level. Gone are the boring PowerPoint presentations and traditional sales demos. Sales, nowadays, doesn't happen in the boardroom; it happens online, in coffee shops, on phone calls, and via video conferences. Millennials are not concerned with being impressed with a PowerPoint presentation, and another millennial understands that better than anyone else.

Millennials Are Tech-Savvy

Millennials have grown up with technology; they have spent more time on their cellphones and laptops than they have invested in anything else. They are intimately familiar with the technology we currently have, and they use it daily. They are more well-informed buyers than the previous generations, and they are open and willing to adapt to new products, technologies, and ideas. A millennial will know exactly what to do in this situation. You, as a millennial, have to think about what you would try and what would make you purchase a product. That is exactly why you can be a very successful network marketer.

Millennials Are Independent Thinkers

Millennials are in a league of their own. They don't mind not following norms, and they are able to think for themselves without the help of others. They have a lot of information on their hands, and their opinions are built by themselves, with not much influence from others. This generation has grown up with independence, and it comprises of independent thinkers. They want solutions to their specific needs, and they won't settle for anything else. Millennials are more socially conscious than the generations before them; hence, they want to be associated with businesses that share the same mindset and values. Social justice and corporate responsibility are very important to them, and that is exactly what a millennial will understand. This is another reason that it might be hard for a baby boomer to sell to a millennial but so easy for a millennial to do the same job.

Millennials Communicate in a Different Way

Millennials are not limited to talking on the phone and face to face. They have a very different preference than previous generations when it comes to communication. For sales companies, that means that they need to alter their way of communication to reflect their buyers' preference. Most millennials prefer emails, texts, and social media conversations over in-person meetings and phone calls. As a millennial, you would be great at communicating with other millennials through text.

Millennials are a great asset to network marketing companies. That is why a lot of the job ads you see would want a young person to fill the vacancy. Companies are even willing to train an individual who possesses the skill of social media and a flair for the field. Network marketing is all about using flair and producing something innovative. Nowadays, network marketing isn't about door-to-door sales. It isn't about throwing a party for your friends and family, to sell them your product. Instead, it is about what you want it to be about. If you want to do it the old fashioned way, go ahead and do it. Or if you want to use phone calls, that will work just fine as well. However, the best way to sell your product and grow your team is through social media. Not only is it more convenient, but you probably have vast knowledge about it as well.

Still think that network marketing isn't for you? Well, continue reading, and you'll understand how wrong you are. You are almost at the finish line! See where you can go from here if not forward! I am going to get one-on-one with you here. I found out about network marketing not too long ago myself, and because of this incredible career, my life changed completely. I had the freedom of thought, time, and even finance. I became my own boss. I had never had that in my life before. I first thought that it was just a con, and that nothing good would come from it. But I had nothing to lose, and while I was working a full-time job, I picked up network marketing as a part-time side-gig. A month went by, and I began making good money from it.

I started giving an hour or two more each week, and I discovered that I was making a lot more than ever before. I have no one telling me what to do, and I can work when I want to. I quickly started taking days off from my work, and I started to give it more time to see how far I could push it. Slowly but surely, I started making more money through network marketing part-time than I was making at my full-time job, where the stress level was very high. That year, I was laid off, but I had faith in myself and my new found profession. After a year, I was making more money. I had more time for myself, my family, and my friends. I was basically enjoying life being my own boss. So, if you are tired of your boss, want to make more money on your own time, or want to feel a sense of satisfaction by doing something worthwhile, then network marketing is something you should dip your feet in.

Setting up and launching your own network marketing business is easier than setting up a brick-and-mortar store. You can basically conduct most of your operations with nothing more than your laptop and a good Wi-Fi connection! It also costs a lot less to start a network marketing business.

On the other hand, traditional brick-and-mortar stores involve a lot more effort and investment at the very outset. That's why so many millennials are opting for network marketing nowadays!

Launching Your Own Network Marketing Business

With an emphasis on selling products instead of signing up new members, you need to enlist with an already established network marketing organization, or start your own from the ground up. If you decide to do it yourself, then you would need to establish a relationship with a wholesaler or manufacturer to turn out your actual product.

The first thing you have to do is:

Find a Niche

Select a product line for your network marketing company, which could be anything. For this purpose, you need to have two things in mind.

You believe in the product and would actually buy it yourself. This way, you won't have problems selling it and trying to convince someone to buy it.

It should have a demand. Not all products are going to have high levels of demand, so you need to be careful in finding a suitable product for your business.

Wholesale Suppliers

The next step is finding a supplier for your product. Think of yourself as a middleman. You are going to take the products of the company and sell them to the consumer. Again, it's easier to find these wholesale suppliers for your network marketing business than for a brick and mortar. That's because you can do most of the work online! There is a website set up for you to find suppliers and everything they do. The National Association of Wholesale Distributors has a website: naw.org. It has everything you need to know about almost every supplier present in the U.S.

Set Price Structure

After you have found your supplier, the next order of business for you is setting a price structure for your business. Set the retail price of your product according to your supplier's recommendations. But establish a good commission structure for your distributor on several different levels. Increase your commission as the sales increase.

Organizational and Managerial Setup

You can install a network marketing commission-payment software. Use your commission-payment software to calculate the commission of all future distributors. Create an instruction manual for all distributors—a well thought out and planned manual that you can give to your other future suppliers. The manual would contain instructions about dealing, a catalog, a price list, and order forms.

Marketing Your Business

There are a lot of ways you can market your business as a millennial. You can use traditional ways of marketing, as well as the latest methods. Of course, you will focus the most on social media. You first have to make a Facebook page, then release videos and posts regarding your business, and promote it for about $5, to reach at least 2000 people. It is the cheapest and most convenient form of advertisement. You can also use Instagram, Twitter, and Tumblr in similar ways. Ads on social media become prominent in little time, as everyone checks their news feeds at least once a day.

The algorithm used by the social media websites would show your page to people who are actually interested in the product you are selling.

You will need the following things to stay on top of your game:

- Wholesale supplier
- Commission payment software
- Instruction manual
- Catalogs
- Sales letters
- Brochures
- Price lists
- Order forms
- Shipping envelopes or boxes
- Shipping labels

One of the biggest benefits that you can reap from network marketing is...

Taking Back Your Life!

I remember sitting at a boring desk job for 8 hours each day, just to go home and think about how I hate my job, before I started out in network marketing. Spending 33% of your day on something that you hate just didn't make sense to me. That was why I took up network marketing, and I am glad that I did. Now, after setting up my own business and my own rules, I have so much freedom to do whatever I want. It feels good not having to say no to something because you have to work. It feels nice to be able to say YES, because you are the boss! Going on a hike in the morning and not worrying about being late is the best feeling in the world! Not fearing that your salary would be deducted if you took a day off because you were sick, is the kind of freedom that I love so much in the field of network marketing.

Following are the in-depth reasons:

Freedom and Flexibility

The hours you work are up to you to pick. You can either work for either 9 hours or only 5 hours in a day; the choice is entirely yours. You can do network marketing part-time while you maintain your full-time job. It has flexible hours, meaning whenever you can give it time. It is not a fixed 9–5 job. So everything lies in your hands, which is the beauty of it. You can start it off as a supplement for your current salary, and soon you, too, can become a six-figure earner like me and many others.

Financial Opportunity

Network marketing is one of the best choices if you're looking to create unlimited earning potential but have little upfront money. The saying, *"You need money to make more money,"* is dead true, but only for conventional businesses. For something so unconventional like network marketing, you barely need anything. Millennials have an entrepreneurial mindset, but they lack the income to make it happen. In network marketing, you need very little upfront money.

If you give network marketing enough time, you can expedite your success from 10 to 15 years, to 3 to 5 years. This business can lead to an ongoing residual income for you. If you build it correctly, you can be paid by royalties or residual income forever.

Fun & Friendship

In this business, you get to choose your own partners and people you work with, unlike at your workplace. You didn't choose your colleagues, and some of them are not at all likable, I understand. For this reason, network marketing is amazing. You get to choose the clients you work with and the people you work alongside. In this way, you can build long-lasting friendships and partnerships.

Great Personal and Professional Growth

You get into network marketing for yourself, not by yourself. You don't have to be alone in this. You are in this for yourself and for your own freedom; you are your own boss, and you can enjoy being in control of your own life. This control allows you to grow personally and professionally. You can do things for yourself. Now when you get up in the morning, you get up for yourself. When you pick up that phone to call clients, you do that for yourself. As Holton Buggs says, *"Most people miss the work part of network marketing."* You will start understanding your purpose and your life better. You grow in confidence and communication! The best part? You earn as you learn! Personal and professional growth opportunities definitely outweigh the paycheck!

Congratulations!

You have finally reached the end of this book.

Isn't it a good feeling, learning something new?

So why not start doing something new in your life, for yourself? Believe in yourself, and take the leap of faith.

Hurry over to MInvasion.com today, to set up your first free coaching call.

Remember, you can do anything!

M.A.D. millennial, you're finally living!

Bibliography

Khadrice Rollins. (2018). What does "Trust the Process" mean? Retrieved from: https://www.si.com/nba/2018/trust-the-process-meaning-philadelphia-76ers-team-motto

Sassy Suite. (2015). How to connect millennials with direct sales and network marketing. Retrieved from: https://www.sassysuite.com/how-to-connect-millennials-with-direct-sales-and-network-marketing/

Richie Norton. (2017). The 14 most destructive millennial myths debunked by Data. Retrieved from: https://medium.com/the-mission/the-14-most-destructive-millennial-myths-debunked-by-data-aa00838eecd6

Made in the USA
Columbia, SC
27 July 2020